Gentle Wilderness

"And after ten years spent in the heart of it,

rejoicing and wondering, bathing in its glorious floods of light, seeing the sunbursts of morning among the icy peaks,

the noonday radiance on the trees and rocks and snow,

the flush of alpenglow,

and a thousand dashing waterfalls

      with their marvelous abundance of irised spray,

it still seems to me above all others

the Range of Light"

"The snow is melting into music . . ."

Gentle Wilderness THE SIERRA NEVADA

Photographs by RICHARD KAUFFMAN   *Text from* JOHN MUIR

Edited by DAVID BROWER

PROMONTORY
PRESS

This edition published in the United States of America in 1981 by
Promontory Press
95 Madison Avenue
New York, New York 10016
By arrangement with Sierra Club Books

Library of Congress Catalog Card Number: 81-81159
ISBN: 0-88394-047-7
Printed in the United States of America

The text from My First Summer in the Sierra *is condensed with the permission of*
Houghton Mifflin Company; © *1911 by John Muir,* © *1939 by Wanda Muir Hannah*

to my mother and father
who have always encouraged my interest
in photography and in wilderness

FOREWORD

What John Muir had to say in *My First Summer in the Sierra* led me, forty years ago, to feel I had already been in the Yosemite High Sierra he was discovering for the first time. Nearly a century after John Muir's first summer, Richard Kauffman has come along with camera instead of notebook to recapture the sense of discovery, and the vividness of what Muir called the Range of Light. Here is the Sierra the way Muir saw it, the way others have seen their first summers confirmed, when they read of Muir's. A cool Sierra wind blows through the photographs, a gentle wind. It is a Sierra illumined by the light of the gentle hours, warm light on a friendly, inviting land.

Is it really gentle wilderness? There is room for argument. Certainly the gentleness of this Sierra wilderness is never soft enough to be cloying. Fear can be mixed with your exhilaration. The passes come impressively high, your breath short, and your pulse rapid. Some of the deepest snows in North America fall there and nothing is gentle about the avalanches when the slopes unload, or about winter temperatures that may drop to fifty-five below. You don't feel very pampered when you are on a half-inch ledge halfway up one of the half-mile-high sheer Yosemite cliffs, or when the March wind finds you and, even though you brace against it with ski poles, flattens you on Mount Lyell's icy shoulder, or when a driving spray drenches you if you venture within a hundred yards of the foot of Vernal Fall in flood, or when a desert sun bakes you at the foot of the Sierra's eastern escarpment, two vertical miles below the summit of Mount Whitney.

Still there is always enough gentleness in the Sierra, or soon will be, when the storm clears or the rough climb ends. No other of the world's great ranges that Mr. Kauffman knows, or that I know, or that so far as we know Muir knew, is as gentle as the Sierra.

If there is to be objection, it is that the Sierra is too gentle—too gentle to counter man's assaults against it. John Muir saw this in his first summer and in the later summers and winters when the Sierra was his address. He dedicated his life to a counterassault on man's misuse of wilderness and wildlife. He helped establish national parks, enlisted support of national leaders in a preservation movement, battled Gifford Pinchot's predominantly utilitarian interest in conservation, wrote and talked and led with exuberant energy—with the same energy that took him through his favorite forests, among the alpine gardens he loved, and on up so many of the Sierra peaks.

He also founded the Sierra Club "to explore, enjoy, and render accessible" the mountain range it was named after. In 1911 he dedicated *First Summer* to the members of the club for their good work.

One of his ideas for rendering the Sierra accessible was a program of summer wilderness outings which he and William E. Colby initiated in 1901. Too many of the places he loved were being lost because too few people knew about them. There would be no hope of sparing Sierra meadows from being overgrazed and devastated by domestic sheep, for instance, unless people saw the damage firsthand and also saw unspoiled meadows so as to evaluate the loss. The giant sequoias were being logged for grape stakes. Hetch Hetchy Valley itself was to be dammed—in the last analysis to produce hydroelectric power for San Francisco. It was not enough to write about the beauty of these places and the tragedy of losing them. People must see for themselves, appraise the danger to the spot on the spot. Informed, devoted defense would ensue.

For sixty-three years since then the concept has worked, modified only slightly. Early in the game Muir had felt that accessibility should include a fairly formidable road net through the High Sierra. Late in the 'twenties the Sierra Club directors were still advocating several trans-Sierra roads they would shudder to think about today. The words "render accessible" were being misunderstood as an argument for mechanized access and were amended out of the bylaws. The emphasis shifted to getting people to know wilderness as wilderness, to travel there by foot, to leave the fewest possible marks, to spare for another generation the opportunity to discover that which they themselves had loved.

There was not yet much concern about what the foot—a man's or a mule's—might do to wilderness. The high country was still fairly empty. As late as 1934 I myself could still spend a month in the Kings-Kern country without seeing anyone but my knapsacking companion. Before our ten-week knapsack survey of the John Muir Trail and the Sierra crest was over, we encountered only a few independent travelers—and an entire Sierra Club High Trip of nearly two hundred people and one hundred pack animals. But even then we had only to walk a mile or two to be in empty mountains again (a summer I described in "Far from the Madding Mules," *Sierra Club Bulletin*, annual magazine number, 1935).

Today a thousand people may walk up the east-side

trail to the summit of Mount Whitney over the Labor Day week end; forty thousand may hit Yosemite Valley over a Memorial Day week end. There is a new dimension in mountain use—"visitation," the National Park Service calls it. Park Service ecologists have now identified a few hot spots in the high country above Kings Canyon and Sequoia national parks, places where recreational erosion exceeds a given camping area's capability of recovering. Human erosion itself is not too noticeable, but the associated grazing, trampling, and littering by packstock is severe. What Muir had objected to in the impact of commercial sheep is now being accomplished by animals hired for pleasure. A Forest Service ranger spent a year studying what sheer numbers were doing along Bear Creek, south of Yosemite, and concluded that large groups of wilderness travelers should be eliminated: don't concentrate use in a few places, but disperse it and build primitive toilets and fireplaces in many parts of the wilderness to encourage the dispersal. Not a hundred people in one spot, but ten people in ten spots, or five in twenty. Meanwhile, back in Washington, his parent agency was arguing before Congress that there was probably already too much wilderness set aside; considering the little use it was getting, it was far more important to expedite the construction of timber-access roads and logging operations into undedicated wilderness and to make sure that dedicated wilderness was as free as possible of commercial trees. Too little use, yet so much use the land suffered; log it and end the debate!

The confusion continues. The big-trip use that Muir had advocated was the easiest target to hit, or to encourage others to hit. It also happens to be the trip that could serve the widest range of physical and financial abilities. The man too old to carry much of a pack, or the child too young to, can still walk a wilderness trail. Packstock can carry the duffel, the food, the camp equipment. Crew members (usually students who can travel fast enough to break one camp late and make the next one early) allow the wilderness visitor maximum time to enjoy the country with minimum housekeeping. If the moves aren't too far, the stock can relay loads, and half the number of stock can serve the same number of people. Four or more wilderness travelers can thus be served per head of packstock—on a moving trip, the kind that gives the visitor the feel of big, continuous wilderness.

Could wilderness be experienced in such a crowd? Could you see the mountains for the people? As a knapsacker I thought not, but changed my mind in the course of spending a year of summer days on Sierra Club High Trips, making careful notes of what happened, checking with Forest Service and National Park Service observers and ecologists, joining with trip leaders and packers in taking the dozens of steps that minimized the impact of people, whether on the wilderness itself or on other people. I was partial then, and still am eight years later, to the moving trip that can give the visitor the feel of a big, continuous wilderness—one in which you can cross pass after pass and know that on the other side you don't drop into civilization, but stay in wilderness instead. In big wilderness you learn how important size itself is to the viability of wilderness. It needs enough buffer to keep its heartland essentially free from the pervasive influences of technology. Such big wilderness is scarce, and is vanishing at the rate of about a million acres a year, chiefly to the chainsaw. People who know it can save it. No one else.

Were Muir alive today he would see the issue clearly and would keep it clear of all the conscious and unconscious confusion. He would know that the choice was not between pristine wilderness and wilderness overused in spots, but between some overuse and no wilderness at all. He would not forget irreplaceable Glen Canyon, hard-hit at some camps along the river, but still not known by enough people to be saved. The Bureau of Reclamation solved the problem of slightly overused campsites by drowning the entire length of the canyon, permanently, with an unnecessary reservoir.

Muir would see what was happening in the Sierra, and would not be fooled by the forces hostile to preservation who now point a diversionary finger at wilderness footprints. He would point out the marks far more damaging than footprints—logging roads, stumps, and trash-clogged streams—that forever killed gentle wilderness on the Kern Plateau because of too little conservationist use. He would note how the real, unbroken wilderness of the High Sierra climax, extending from the Tioga Road in Yosemite down to the Kern, is still vulnerable: a corridor for a needless trans-Sierra road is relentlessly being kept open at Mammoth Pass, and another south of Whitney Meadows. Because there had been too little use, Muir would observe, the wilderness of Vermilion Valley and of a beautiful basin in the North Fork of the Kings had been drowned by power reservoirs—in a day when hydroelectric power means less and less and unspoiled recreation places mean more and more. Muir would not have been impressed by tears about footprints in eyes that winked at mechanized scooters snorting over wilderness trails.

I am sure that John Muir would still believe that firsthand knowledge of places is vital to their survival and that their survival is vital to man. He needs places where he can be reminded that civilization is only a thin veneer over the deep evolutionary flow of things that built him.

Let wilderness live, and it would always tell him truth.

For all the losses since John Muir's time, an invaluable resource still lives. Much of the Sierra wilderness is essentially what it was half a century ago, altered only by natural succession. The favorite, untouched high places are a constant that can reassure a man. So is the roll of familiar things you pass on your way up the heights—the oak savannah, the digger pines, the orderly succession of ponderosa, incense cedar, sugar pine, the firs, then the denizens of timberline. One trouble these days is that you have to call the roll of friends too fast. Speed and the wide highway have brought a deprivation, for the right reason perhaps, but in the wrong places. Speed shrinks wilderness, and there wasn't really enough in Muir's day to serve all those who followed him to California or who will one day be here to look or to live.

Even as in Muir's time, the Sierra Club's purpose is still to gather together people from all over who know how important it is that there should always be some land wild and free. They are needed to counter the rationalizations of the highway builders, and dam and logging-road builders, who would slice through and dismember the wilderness. The purpose of this book is to remind everyone (to paraphrase Newton Drury) that neither California nor the rest of America is rich enough to lose any more of the Gentle Wilderness or poor enough to need to.

*　*　*

We have taken a few liberties with *First Summer*. It contained, as journals do, some repetition we thought we could omit: daily notes on the weather, duplicate descriptions of clouds, and periodic lists of plants seen. A good many sheep have gone, and a few Indians. Some of Muir's favorite adjectives in the journal have been thinned out, even as he himself thinned them in his later writings. We left danglers and fused participles the way the journal had them. We had a difference of opinion about how much pathetic fallacy should be left in. It is easy to attribute human qualities to other living things if you have been a long time away from other people, and Muir was. All in all, the changes are minor, and do not diminish the sense of discovery in what Muir wrote in his journal.

Richard Kauffman did not have either Muir or *First Summer* in mind in the period of years over which he made the photographs. Nevertheless he saw and photographed exceedingly well just what Muir had seen and described. Mr. Kauffman was up and down the Sierra, while in *First Summer* Muir merely crossed the Yosemite Sierra to Mono Lake and returned to the foothills before autumn was fairly underway. Opposite Muir's writing, or interspersed in sequence as appropriate, we have placed photographs that have the spirit or life zone Muir was talking about, but they may show a place a hundred miles away.

The Muir quotations in italics, including the quotation in the expanded frontispiece, are the only ones that do not come from *My First Summer in the Sierra*.

On behalf of the Sierra Club, I should like to acknowledge deep gratitude to: Richard Kauffman, not only for the beauty of his work, but also for his having generously contributed it to the club; to John Gregg, who condensed *First Summer* but let me restore some lines I was too attached to to let go; to my wife, Anne, whose sense of content, composition, and design underlies my own to say the least; to the members of the Publications Committee and the club directors who foresaw what this book would be and supported it; to the graphic arts people who made it what these people had foreseen, with special thanks to all the patient individuals who made back most of the time I lost in getting material to them; and to Paul Brooks and Houghton-Mifflin, the publishers of John Muir's writing for so many years.

We are mindful, too, of the earlier generosity of people who helped the club build its revolving Publications Fund which, revolving once again, was ready for the major investment this book entailed: the Belvedere Scientific Fund and Nancy and Kenneth Bechtel; Walter A. Starr; the late Inez Mexía, Marion Randall Parsons, and Max McGraw; and I add my own gratitude to all who have encouraged the club's publishing program, especially the exhibit-format series, and who with their support and suggestions have helped the Sierra Club broaden the understanding of what wildness means to civilized man.

More than anything, we hope the series will do something lasting for wilderness. Man needs to save enough of it, what he knows viscerally is enough without waiting for all the statistics. Man can safely assume that for all his shortcomings, he is bright enough to carry on his civilization on the 95 per cent or so of the land he has already disrupted. He is wise enough to recognize that he will not have a bright land, nor really serve himself well, if he hurries to disrupt that last five per cent on the pretext that progress will otherwise cease. It won't. It will cease, however, if we cannot be kind enough to tomorrow's men to leave for them, in big wilderness, a chance to seek answers to questions we have not yet learned how to ask.

DAVID BROWER

Berkeley, California
November 1, 1964

CONTENTS

EIGHTY COLOR PLATES

NOTES ON THE PHOTOGRAPHS AND PLATES

Learning some of the techniques of color photography and then attempting to use these techniques creatively has been a rewarding experience for me and one that has filled many hours of my life with pleasure. During the last thirty years I have had the fortune to see tremendous developments in this field—developments which transformed color photography from a scientific curiosity to an everyday tool of art and industry.

My early experiments with additive screen processes resulted in transparencies that had to be held to the light to be viewed. However, my goal then, as today, was to produce color prints on paper. The mid-1930's saw the development of processes and equipment which, though often difficult and time-consuming, did achieve this goal. The beam-splitting three-color camera was costly and cumbersome to use, but when the separation negatives that it produced were properly made and then skillfully printed by the Carbro process, the results were at least as fine as anything produced now.

The original color prints that form the basis of this book were all made by the Carbro process—a process permitting tonal values that range from delicate highlight to richest, deepest black. Undoubtedly this process is the only color process ever invented that yields a print that retains its original color quality even when exposed to light over long periods of time. However, the specialized camera equipment mentioned above had been superseded by conventional lighter weight cameras before the pictures in this book were taken. Thus, with my burden lightened, I found it easier to roam the Sierra.

The film used for all the pictures in this book was color negative film, either Kodacolor or Ektacolor. From these films I made color separation negatives and then printed them by the Carbro process. I have never used positive color film (such as Kodachrome or Ektachrome) for making color prints as I feel the results, by comparison, are inferior.

When the time came to make the plates for this book, I was confronted with a serious problem. Lithographers and trade platemakers, proficient as they might be in making plates from positive color film, had no experience in making plates from color negatives. I did not wish to have the platemaker work from my color prints as I felt that there would be a quality loss compared to working from the original color negative. I therefore purchased a 200 line magenta contact screen to experiment in my dark room with the production of lithograph halftone separations from color negatives. I was delighted to find upon making lithograph press proofs of these experiments, that the results closely approximated the original Carbro print. With these experiments behind me, I proceeded to make all the color plates from which this book was printed. My home dark room is well-equipped but boasts no unusual equipment except the contact screen, the vacuum pump, and the register board used with the pump. I used absolutely no handwork or color correcting in making these plates, as is customary in lithographic reproduction. (Lithographic artists did, however, remove the pinholes, scratches, and blemishes that tend to creep into one's work.) In my opinion it was the use of color negatives rather than color positive film that eliminated the need for handwork in preparing the plates for the book.   R.K.

PHOTOGRAPHS

MY FIRST SUMMER IN THE SIERRA

*"Walk away quietly in any direction
and taste the freedom of the mountaineer.
Camp out among the grass and gentians
of glacier meadows, in craggy garden nooks . . ."*

Through the Foothills

In the great Central Valley of California there are only two seasons—spring and summer. The spring begins with the first rainstorm, which usually falls in November. In a few months the wonderful flowery vegetation is in full bloom, and by the end of May it is dead and dry and crisp, as if every plant had been roasted in an oven.

Then the lolling, panting flocks and herds are driven to the high, cool, green pastures of the Sierra. I was longing for the mountains about this time, but money was scarce and I couldn't see how a bread supply was to be kept up. While I was anxiously brooding on the bread problem, so troublesome to wanderers, and trying to believe that I might learn to live like the wild animals, gleaning nourishment here and there from seeds, berries, etc., sauntering and climbing in joyful independence of money or baggage, Mr. Delaney, a sheepowner, for whom I had worked a few weeks, called on me, and offered to engage me to go with his shepherd and flock to the headwaters of the Merced and Tuolumne Rivers—the very region I had most in mind. I was in the mood to accept work of any kind that would take me into the mountains whose treasures I had tasted last summer in the Yosemite region. The flock, he explained, would be moved gradually higher through the successive forest belts as the snow melted, stopping for a few weeks at the best places we came to. These I thought would be good centers of observation from which I might be able to make many telling excursions within a radius of eight or ten miles of the camps to learn something of the plants, animals, and rocks; for he assured me that I should be left perfectly free to follow my studies. I judged, however, that I was in no way the right man for the place, and freely explained my shortcomings, confessing that I was wholly unacquainted with the topography of the upper mountains, the streams that would have to be crossed, and the wild sheep-eating animals, etc.; in short that, what with bears, coyotes, rivers, canyons, and thorny, bewildering chaparral, I feared that half or more of his flock would be lost. Fortunately these shortcomings seemed insignificant to Mr. Delaney. The main thing, he said, was to have a man about the camp whom he could trust to see that the shepherd did his duty, and he assured me that the difficul-

ties that seemed so formidable at a distance would vanish as we went on; encouraging me further by saying that the shepherd would do all the herding, that I could study plants and rocks and scenery as much as I liked, and that he would himself accompany us to the first main camp and make occasional visits to our higher ones to replenish our store of provisions and see how we prospered. Therefore I concluded to go, though still fearing, when I saw the silly sheep bouncing one by one through the narrow gate of the home corral to be counted, that of the two thousand and fifty many would never return.

I was fortunate in getting a fine St. Bernard dog for a companion. His master, a hunter with whom I was slightly acquainted, came to me as soon as he heard that I was going to spend the summer in the Sierra and begged me to take his favorite dog, Carlo, with me, for he feared that if he were compelled to stay all summer on the plains the fierce heat might be the death of him. "I think I can trust you to be kind to him," he said, "and I am sure he will be good to you. He knows all about the mountain animals, will guard the camp, assist in managing the sheep, and in every way be found able and faithful." Carlo knew we were talking about him, watched our faces, and listened so attentively that I fancied he understood us. Calling him by name, I asked him if he was willing to go with me. He looked me in the face with eyes expressing wonderful intelligence, then turned to his master, and after permission was given by a wave of the hand toward me and a farewell patting caress, he quietly followed me as if he perfectly understood all that had been said and had known me always.

June 3, 1869

This morning provisions, campkettles, blankets, plant-press, etc., were packed on two horses, the flock headed for the tawny foothills, and away we sauntered in a cloud of dust: Mr. Delaney, bony and tall, with sharply hacked profile like Don Quixote, leading the pack-horses, Billy, the proud shepherd, a Chinaman and a Digger Indian to assist in driving for the first few days in the brushy foothills, and myself with notebook tied to my belt.

The home ranch from which we set out is on the south side of the Tuolumne River near French Bar, where the foothills of metamorphic gold-bearing slates dip below the stratified deposits of the Central Valley. We had not gone more than a mile before some of the old leaders of the flock showed by the eager, inquiring way they ran and looked ahead that they were thinking of the high pastures they had enjoyed last summer. Soon the whole flock seemed to be hopefully excited, the mothers calling their lambs, the lambs replying in tones wonderfully human, their fondly quavering calls interrupted now and then by hastily snatched mouthfuls of withered grass. Amid all this seeming babel of baas as they streamed over the hills every mother and child recognized each other's voice. In case a tired lamb, half asleep in the smothering dust, should fail to answer, its mother would come running back through the flock toward the spot whence its last response was heard, and refused to be comforted until she found it, the one of a thousand, though to our eyes and ears all seemed alike.

The flock traveled at the rate of about a mile an hour, outspread in the form of an irregular triangle, about a hundred yards wide at the base, and a hundred and fifty yards long, with a crooked, ever-changing point made up of the strongest foragers, called the "leaders," which, with the most active of those scattered along the ragged sides of the "main body," hastily explored nooks in the rocks and bushes for grass and leaves; the lambs and feeble old mothers dawdling in the rear were called the "tail end."

About noon the heat was hard to bear; the poor sheep panted pitifully and tried to stop in the shade of every tree they came to, while we gazed with eager longing through the dim burning glare toward the snowy mountains and streams, though not one was in sight. The landscape is only wavering foothills roughened here and there with bushes and trees and outcropping masses of slate. The trees, mostly the blue oak (*Quercus Douglasii*), are about thirty to forty feet high, with pale blue-green leaves and white bark, sparsely planted on the thinnest soil or in crevices of rocks beyond the reach of grass fires. The slates in many places rise abruptly through the tawny grass in sharp lichen-covered slabs like tombstones in deserted burying-grounds. With the exception of the oak and four or five species of manzanita and ceanothus, the vegetation of the foothills is mostly the same as that of the plains. I saw this region in the early spring, when it was a charming landscape garden full of birds and bees and flowers. Now the scorching weather makes everything dreary. The ground is full of cracks, lizards glide about on the rocks, and ants in amazing numbers, whose tiny sparks of life

only burn the brighter with the heat, fairly quiver with unquenchable energy as they run in long lines to fight and gather food. How it comes that they do not dry to a crisp in a few seconds' exposure to such sun-fire is marvelous. A few rattlesnakes lie coiled in out-of-the-way places, but are seldom seen. Magpies and crows, usually so noisy, are silent now, standing in mixed flocks on the ground beneath the best shade trees, with bills wide open and wings drooped, too breathless to speak; the quails also are trying to keep in the shade about the few tepid alkaline water-holes; cottontail rabbits are running from shade to shade among the ceanothus brush, and occasionally the long-eared hare is seen cantering gracefully across the wider openings.

After a short noon rest in a grove, the poor dust-choked flock was again driven ahead over the brushy hills, but the dim roadway we had been following faded away just where it was most needed, compelling us to stop to look about us and get our bearings. The Chinaman seemed to think we were lost, and chattered in pidgin English concerning the abundance of "litty stick" (chaparral), while the Indian silently scanned the billowy ridges and gulches for openings. Pushing through the thorny jungle, we at length discovered a road trending toward Coulterville, which we followed until an hour before sunset, when we reached a dry ranch and camped for the night.

Camping in the foothills with a flock of sheep is simple and easy, but far from pleasant. The sheep were allowed to pick what they could find in the neighborhood until after sunset, watched by the shepherd, while the others gathered wood, made a fire, cooked, unpacked and fed the horses, etc. About dusk the weary sheep were gathered on the highest open spot near camp, where they willingly bunched close together, and after each mother had found her lamb and suckled it, all lay down and required no attention until morning.

Supper was announced by the call, "Grub!" Each with a tin plate helped himself direct from the pots and pans while chatting about such camp studies as sheep-feed, mines, coyotes, bears, or adventures during the memorable gold days of pay dirt. The Indian kept in the background, saying never a word, as if he belonged to another species. The meal finished, the dogs were fed, the smokers smoked by the fire, and under the influences of fullness and tobacco the calm that settled on their faces seemed almost divine, something like the mellow meditative glow portrayed on the countenances of saints. Then suddenly, as if awakening from a dream, each with a sign or a grunt knocked the ashes out of his pipe, yawned, gazed at the fire a few moments, said, "Well, I believe I'll turn in," and straightway vanished beneath his blankets. The fire smouldered and flickered an hour to two longer; the stars shone brighter; coons, coyotes, and owls stirred the silence here and there, while crickets and hylas made a cheerful, continuous music, so fitting and full that it seemed a part of the very body of the night. The only discordance came from a snoring sleeper, and the coughing sheep with dust in their throats. In the starlight the flock looked like a big gray blanket.

June 4

The camp was astir at daybreak; coffee, bacon, and beans formed the breakfast, followed by quick dish-washing and packing. A general bleating began about sunrise. As soon as a mother ewe arose, her lamb came bounding and bunting for its breakfast, and after the thousand youngsters had been suckled the flock began to nibble and spread. The restless wethers with ravenous appetites were the first to move, but dared not go far from the main body. Billy and the Indian and the Chinaman kept them headed along the weary road, and allowed them to pick up what little they could find on a breadth of about a quarter of a mile. But as several flocks had already gone ahead of us, scarce a leaf, green or dry, was left; therefore the starving flock had to be hurried on over the bare, hot hills to the nearest of the green pastures, about twenty or thirty miles from here.

The pack-animals were led by Don Quixote, a heavy rifle over his shoulder intended for bears and wolves. This day has been as hot and dusty as the first, leading over gently sloping brown hills, with mostly the same vegetation, excepting the strange-looking Sabine pine (*Pinus Sabiniana*), which here forms small groves or is scattered among the blue oaks. The trunk divides at a height of fifteen or twenty feet into two or more stems, outleaning or nearly upright, with many straggling branches and long gray needles, casting but little shade. In general appearance this tree looks more like a palm than a pine. The cones are about six or seven inches long, about five in diameter, very heavy, and last long after they fall, so that the ground beneath the trees is covered with them. They make fine resiny, light-giving camp-fires, next to ears of Indian corn the most beautiful fuel I've ever seen. The nuts, the Don tells me, are gathered in large quantities by the Digger Indians for food. They are about as large and hard-shelled as hazelnuts—food and fire fit for the gods from the same fruit.

June 5

This morning a few hours after setting out with the crawling sheep-cloud, we gained the summit of the first well-defined bench on the mountain-flank at Pino Blanco. The Sabine pines interest me greatly. They are so airy and strangely palm-like I was eager to sketch them, and was in a fever of excitement without accomplishing much. I managed to halt long enough, however, to make a tolerably fair sketch of Pino Blanco peak from the southwest side, where there is a small field and vineyard irrigated by a stream that makes a pretty fall on its way down a gorge by the roadside.

After gaining the open summit of this first bench, feeling the natural exhilaration due to the slight elevation of

Horseshoe Bend, Merced River

a thousand feet or so, and the hopes excited concerning the outlook to be obtained, a magnificent section of the Merced Valley at what is called Horseshoe Bend came full in sight—a glorious wilderness that seemed to be calling with a thousand songful voices. Bold, down-sweeping slopes, feathered with pines and clumps of manzanita with sunny, open spaces between them, make up most of the foreground; the middle and background present fold beyond fold of finely modeled hills and ridges rising into mountain-like masses in the distance, all covered with a shaggy growth of chaparral. . . . As far as the eye can reach it extends, a heaving, swelling sea of green as regular and continuous as that produced by the heaths of Scotland. The sculpture of the landscape is as striking in its main lines as in its lavish richness of detail. . . . The whole landscape showed design, like man's noblest sculptures. How wonderful the power of its beauty! Gazing awestricken, I might have left everything for it. Glad, endless work would then be mine tracing the forces that have brought forth its features, its rocks and plants and animals and glorious weather. . . .

The evening . . . is cool, calm, cloudless, and full of a

kind of lightning I have never seen before—white glowing cloud-shaped masses down among the trees and bushes, like quick-throbbing fireflies in the Wisconsin meadows rather than the so-called "wild fire." The spreading hairs of the horses' tails and sparks from our blankets show how highly charged the air is.

June 6

We are now on what may be called the second bench or plateau of the Range, after making many small ups and downs over belts of hill-waves, with, of course, corres-

On Second Bench, near Greeley's Mill

ponding changes in the vegetation. In open spots many of the lowland compositæ are still to be found, and some of the Mariposa tulips and other conspicuous members of the lily family; but the characteristic blue oak of the foot-hills is left below, and its place is taken by a fine large species (*Quercus Californica*) with deeply lobed deciduous leaves. . . . Here also at a height of about twenty-five hundred feet we came to the edge of the great coniferous forest, made up mostly of yellow pine with just a few sugar pines. We are now in the mountains and they are in us, kindling enthusiasm, making every nerve quiver, filling every pore and cell of us. . . .

Through a meadow opening in the pine woods I see snowy peaks about the headwaters of the Merced above Yosemite. How near they seem and how clear their outlines on the blue air, or rather *in* the blue air; for they seem to be saturated with it. . . .

During the afternoon we passed a fine meadow bounded by stately pines, mostly the arrowy yellow pine, with here and there a noble sugar pine, its feathery arms outspread above the spires of its companion species in marked contrast; a glorious tree, its cones fifteen to twenty inches long, swinging like tassels at the ends of the branches with superb ornamental effect. Saw some logs of this species at the Greeley Mill. They are round and regular as if turned

in a lathe, excepting the butt cuts, which have a few buttressing projections. The fragrance of the sugary sap is delicious and scents the mill and lumber yard. How beautiful the ground beneath this pine thickly strewn with slender needles and grand cones, and the piles of cone-scales, seed-wings and shells around the instep of each tree where the squirrels have been feasting! . . . The yellow pine cones and those of most other species and genera are held upside down on the ground by the Douglas squirrel, and turned around gradually until stripped, while he sits usually with his back to a tree, probably for safety. Strange to say, he never seems to get himself smeared with gum, not even his paws or whiskers. . . .

We are now approaching the region of clouds and cool streams. Magnificent white cumuli appeared about noon above the Yosemite region,—floating fountains refreshing the glorious wilderness. . . . No rock landscape is more varied in sculpture, none more delicately modeled than these landscapes of the sky; domes and peaks rising, swelling, white as finest marble and firmly outlined, a most impressive manifestation of world building. Every rain-cloud, however fleeting, leaves its mark, not only on trees and flowers whose pulses are quickened, and on the replenished streams and lakes, but also on the rocks are its marks engraved whether we can see them or not. . . .

Azalea . . . grows beside cool steams hereabouts and much higher in the Yosemite region. We found it this evening in bloom a few miles above Greeley's Mill, where we are camped for the night. It is closely related to the rhododendrons, is very showy and fragrant, and everybody must like it not only for itself but for the shady alders and willows, ferny meadows, and living water associated with it.

Another conifer was met to-day—incense cedar (*Libocedrus decurrens*), a large tree with warm yellow-green foliage in flat plumes like those of arborvitae, bark cinnamon-colored, and as the boles of the old trees are without limbs they make striking pillars in the woods where the sun chances to shine on them—a worthy companion of the kingly sugar and yellow pines. I feel strangely attracted to this tree. The brown close-grained wood, as well as the small scale-like leaves, is fragrant, and the flat over-lapping plumes make fine beds, and must shed the rain well. It would be delightful to be storm-bound beneath one of these noble, hospitable, inviting old trees, its broad sheltering arms bent down like a tent, incense rising from the fire made from its dry fallen branches, and a hearty wind chanting overhead. But the weather is calm to-night, and our camp is only a sheep camp. We are near the North Fork of the Merced. The night wind is telling the wonders of the upper mountains, their snow fountains and gardens, forests and groves; even their topography is in its tones. And the stars, . . . how bright they are now that we have climbed above the lowland dust! The horizon is bounded and adorned by a spiry wall of pines, every tree harmoniously related to every other; definite symbols, . . . hieroglyphics written with sunbeams. . . .

June 7

The sheep were sick last night, and many of them are still far from well, hardly able to leave camp, coughing, groaning, looking wretched and pitiful, all from eating the leaves of the blessed azalea. So at least say the shepherd and the Don. Having had but little grass since they left the plains, they are starving, and so eat anything green they can get. "Sheep-men" call azalea "sheep-poison," and wonder what the Creator was thinking about when he made it—so desperately does sheep business blind and degrade, though supposed to have a refining influence in the good old days we read of. The California sheep owner is in haste to get rich, and often does, now that pasturage costs nothing, while the climate is so favorable that no winter food supply, shelter-pens, or barns are required. Therefore large flocks may be kept at slight expense, and large profits realized, the money invested doubling, it is claimed, every other year. This quickly acquired wealth usually creates desire for more. Then indeed the wool is drawn close down over the poor fellow's eyes, dimming or shutting out almost everything worth seeing.

As for the shepherd, his case is still worse, especially in winter when he lives alone in a cabin. For, though stimulated at times by hopes of one day owning a flock and getting rich like his boss, he at the same time is likely to be degraded by the life he leads, and seldom reaches the dignity or advantage—or disadvantage—of ownership. The degradation in his case has for cause one not far to seek. He is solitary most of the year, and solitude to most people seems hard to bear. He seldom has much good mental work or recreation in the way of books. Coming into his dingy hovel-cabin at night, stupidly weary, he finds nothing to balance and level his life with the universe. No, after his dull drag all day after the sheep, he must get his supper; he is likely to slight this task and try to satisfy his hunger with whatever comes handy. Perhaps no bread is baked; then he just makes a few grimy flapjacks in his unwashed fryingpan, boils a handful of tea, and perhaps fries a few strips of rusty bacon. Usually there are dried peaches or apples in the cabin, but he hates to be bothered with the cooking of them, just swallows the bacon and flapjacks, and depends on the genial stupefaction of tobacco for the rest. Then to bed, often without removing the clothing worn during the day. Of course his health suffers, reacting on his mind; and seeing nobody for weeks or months, he finally becomes semi-insane or wholly so.

The shepherd in Scotland seldom thinks of being anything but a shepherd. He has probably descended from a race of shepherds and inherited a love and aptitude for the business almost as marked as that of his collie. He has but a small flock to look after, sees his family and neighbors, has time for reading in fine weather, and often carries books to the fields with which he may converse with kings. The oriental shepherd, we read, called his sheep by name; they knew his voice and followed him. The flocks must have been small and easily managed, allowing piping on the hills and ample leisure for reading and thinking. But whatever the blessings of sheep-culture in other times and countries, the California shepherd, as far as I've seen or heard, is never quite sane for any considerable time. Of all Nature's voices baa is about all he hears. Even the howls and ki-yis of coyotes might be blessings if well heard, but he hears them only through a blur of mutton and wool, and they do him no good.

The sick sheep are getting well, and the shepherd is discoursing on the various poisons lurking in these high pastures—azalea, kalmia, alkali. After crossing the North Fork of the Merced we turned to the left toward Pilot Peak, and made a considerable ascent on a rocky, brush-covered ridge to Brown's Flat, where for the first time since leaving the plains the flock is enjoying plenty of green grass. Mr. Delaney intends to seek a permanent camp somewhere in the neighborhood, to last several weeks.

Before noon we passed Bower Cave, a delightful marble palace, not dark and dripping, but filled with sunshine, which pours into it through its wide-open mouth facing the south. It has a fine, deep, clear little lake with mossy banks embowered with broad-leaved maples, all under ground, wholly unlike anything I have seen in the cave line even in Kentucky, where a large part of the State is honeycombed with caves. This curious specimen of subterranean scenery is located on a belt of marble that is said to extend from the north end of the Range to the extreme south. Many other caves occur on the belt, but none like this, as far as I have learned, combining as it does sunny outdoor brightness and vegetation with the crystalline beauty of the underworld. It is claimed by a Frenchman, who has fenced and locked it, placed a boat on the lakelet and seats on the mossy bank under the maple trees, and charges a dollar admission fee. Being on one of the ways to the Yosemite Valley, a good many tourists visit it during the travel months of summer, regarding it as an interesting addition to their Yosemite wonders.

Poison oak or poison ivy (*Rhus diversiloba*), both as a bush and a scrambler up trees and rocks, is common throughout the foothill region up to a height of at least three thousand feet above the sea. It is somewhat troublesome to most travelers, inflaming the skin and eyes, but blends harmoniously with its companion plants. . . . I have often-times found the curious twining lily (*Stropholirion Californicum*) climbing its branches, showing no fear but rather congenial companionship. Sheep eat it without apparent ill effects; so do horses to some extent, though not fond of it, and to many persons it is harmless. Like most other things not apparently useful to man, it has few friends, and the blind question, "Why was it made?" goes on and on with never a guess that first of all it might have been made for itself.

Brown's Flat is a shallow fertile valley on the top of the divide between the North Fork of the Merced and Bull Creek, commanding magnificent views in every direction. Here the adventurous pioneer David Brown made his headquarters for many years, dividing his time between gold-hunting and bear-hunting. Where could lonely hunter find a better solitude? Game in the woods, gold in the rocks, health and exhilaration in the air, while the colors and cloud furniture of the sky are ever inspiring through all sorts of weather. Though sternly practical, like most pioneers, old David seems to have been uncommonly fond of scenery. Mr. Delaney, who knew him well, tells me that he dearly loved to climb to the summit of a command-ing ridge to gaze abroad over the forest to the snow-clad peaks and sources of the rivers, and over the foreground valleys and gulches to note where miners were at work or claims were abandoned, judging by smoke from cabins and camp-fires, the sounds of axes, etc.; and when a rifle-shot was heard, to guess who was the hunter, whether Indian or some poacher on his wide domain. . . . It was as a bear-hunter that Brown became famous. His hunting method, as described by Mr. Delaney, who had passed many a night with him in his lonely cabin and learned his stories, was simply to go slowly and silently through the best bear pastures, with his dog and rifle and a few pounds of flour, until he found a fresh track and then follow it to the death, paying no heed to the time required. Wherever the bear went he followed. . . . When high open points were reached, the likeliest places were carefully scanned. The time of year enabled the hunter to determine approxi-mately where the bear would be found,—in the spring and early summer on open spots about the banks of streams and springy places eating grass and clover and lupines, or in dry meadows feasting on strawberries; toward the end of summer, on dry ridges, feasting on manzanita berries, sitting on his haunches, pulling down the laden branches with his paws, and pressing them together so as to get good compact mouthfuls however much mixed with twigs and leaves; in the Indian summer, beneath the pines, chewing the cones cut off by the squirrels, or occasionally climbing a tree to gnaw and break off the fruitful branches. . . ." When the hot scent showed the dangerous game was nigh, a long halt was made, and the intricacies of the topography and vegetation leisurely scanned to catch a glimpse of the shaggy wanderer, or to at least determine where he was most likely to be.

"Whenever," said the hunter, "I saw a bear before it saw me I had no trouble in killing it. I just studied the lay of the land and got to leeward of it no matter how far around I had to go, and then worked up to within a few hundred yards or so, at the foot of a tree that I could easily climb, but too small for the bear to climb. Then I looked well to the condition of my rifle, took off my boots so as to climb well if necessary, and waited until the bear turned its side in clear view when I could make a sure or at least a good shot. In case it showed fight I climbed out of reach. But bears are slow and awkward with their eyes, and being to leeward of them they could not scent me, and I often got in a second shot before they noticed the smoke. . . ."

Brown had left his mountain home ere we arrived, but a considerable number of Digger Indians still linger in their cedar-bark huts on the edge of the flat. They were attracted in the first place by the white hunter whom they had learned to respect, and to whom they looked for guidance and protection against their enemies the Pah Utes, who sometimes made raids across from the east side of the Range to plunder the stores of the comparatively feeble Diggers and steal their wives.

In Camp on the North Fork of the Merced

The sheep, now grassy and goodnatured, slowly nibbled their way down into the valley of the North Fork of the Merced at the foot of Pilot Peak Ridge to the place selected by the Don for our first central camp, a picturesque hopper-shaped hollow formed by converging hill slopes at a bend of the river. Here racks for dishes and provisions were made in the shade of the river-bank trees, and beds of fern fronds, cedar plumes, and various flowers, each to the taste of its owner, and a corral back on the open flat for the wool.

June 9

How deep our sleep last night in the mountain's heart, beneath the trees and stars, hushed by solemn-sounding waterfalls and many small soothing voices in sweet accord whispering peace! And our first pure mountain day, warm, calm, cloudless,—how immeasurable it seems, how serenely wild! I can scarcely remember its beginning. Along the river, over the hills, in the ground, in the sky, spring work is going on with joyful enthusiasm, new life, new beauty, unfolding, unrolling in glorious exuberant extravagance,—new birds in their nests, new winged creatures in the air, and new leaves, new flowers, spreading, shining, rejoicing everywhere. . . .

The sheep do not take kindly to their new pastures, perhaps from being too closely hemmed in by the hills. They are never fully at rest. Last night they were frightened, probably by bears or coyotes prowling and planning for a share of the grand mass of mutton.

June 10

Very warm. We get water for the camp from a rock basin at the foot of a picturesque cascading reach of the river where it is well stirred and made lively without being beaten into dusty foam. The rock here is black metamorphic slate, worn into smooth knobs in the stream channels, contrasting with the fine gray and white cascading water as it glides and glances and falls in lace-like sheets and braided overfolding currents. . . . Near camp the trees arch over from bank to bank, making a leafy tunnel full of soft

subdued light, through which the young river sings and shines like a happy living creature.

Heard a few peals of thunder from the upper Sierra, and saw firm white bossy cumuli rising back of the pines. This was about noon.

June 11

On one of the eastern branches of the river discovered some charming cascades with a pool at the foot of each of them. White dashing water, a few bushes and tufts of carex on ledges leaning over with fine effect, and large orange lilies assembled in superb groups on fertile soil-beds beside the pools.

There are no large meadows or grassy plains near camp to supply lasting pasture for our thousands of busy nibblers. The main dependence is ceanothus brush on the hills and tufted grass patches here and there, with lupines and pea-vines among the flowers on sunny open spaces. Large areas have already been stripped bare, or nearly so, compelling the poor hungry wool bundles to scatter far and wide, keeping the shepherds and dogs at the top of their speed to hold them within bounds. Mr. Delaney has gone back to the plains, taking the Indian and Chinaman with him, leaving instruction to keep the flock here or hereabouts until his return, which he promised would not be long delayed.

How fine the weather is! Nothing more celestial can I conceive. How gently the winds blow! Scarce can these tranquil air-currents be called winds. . . .

June 12

A slight sprinkle of rain—large drops far apart, falling with hearty pat and plash on leaves and stones and into the mouths of the flowers. Cumuli rising to the eastward. How beautiful their pearly bosses! How well they harmonize with the upswelling rocks beneath them. Mountains of the sky, solid-looking, finely sculptured, their richly varied topography wonderfully defined. Never before have I seen clouds so substantial looking in form and texture. Nearly every day toward noon they rise with visible swelling motion as if new worlds were being created. . . . One may fancy the clouds themselves are plants, springing up in the skyfields at the call of the sun, growing in beauty until they reach their prime, scattering rain and hail like berries and seeds, then wilting and dying.

Mountain live oak

The mountain live oak, common here and a thousand feet or so higher, is like the live oak of Florida, not only in general appearance, foliage, bark, and wide-branching habit, but in its tough, knotty, unwedgeable wood. Standing alone with plenty of elbow room, the largest trees are about seven to eight feet in diameter near the ground, sixty feet high, and as wide or wider across the head. . . . Some of the trees have hardly any main trunk, dividing near the ground into large wide-spreading limbs, and these, dividing again and again, terminate in long, drooping, cord-like branchlets, many of which reach nearly to the ground, while a dense canopy of short, shining, leafy branchlets forms a round head which looks something like a cumulus cloud when the sunshine is pouring over it. . . .

June 13

Another glorious Sierra day in which one seems to be dissolved and absorbed and sent pulsing onward we know not where. Life seems neither long nor short, and we take no more heed to save time or make haste than do the trees and stars. This is true freedom, a good practical sort of immortality. . . .

A good many herbaceous plants come thus far up the mountains from the plains, and are now in flower, two months later than their lowland relatives. . . . Most of the ferns are in their prime,—rock ferns on the sunny hillsides, cheilanthes, pellæa, gymnogramme; woodwardia, aspidium, woodsia along the stream banks, and the common *Pteris aquilina* on sandy flats. This last, however common, is here making shows of strong, exuberant, abounding beauty to set the botanist wild with admiration. I measured some scarce full grown that are more than seven feet high. Though the commonest and most widely distributed of all the ferns, I might almost say that I never saw it before. The broad-shouldered fronds held high on smooth stout stalks growing close together, overleaning and overlapping, make a complete ceiling, beneath which one may walk erect over several acres without being seen, as if beneath a roof. And how soft and lovely the light streaming through this living ceiling, revealing the arching branching ribs and veins of the fronds as the framework of countless panes of pale green and yellow plant-glass nicely fitted together—a fairyland created out of the commonest fernstuff.

The smaller animals wander about as if in a tropical forest. I saw the entire flock of sheep vanish at one side of a patch and reappear a hundred yards farther on at the other, their progress betrayed only by the jerking and trembling of the fronds; and strange to say very few of the stout woody stalks were broken. I sat a long time beneath the tallest fronds, and never enjoyed anything in the way of a bower of wild leaves more strangely impressive. . . . Yet this very day I saw a shepherd pass through one of the finest of them without betraying more feeling than his sheep. "What do you think of these grand ferns?" I asked. "Oh, they're only d——d big brakes," he replied.

Lizards of every temper, style, and color dwell here. . . . they dart about on the hot rocks, swift as dragon-flies. The eye can hardly follow them; but they never make long-sustained runs, usually only about ten or twelve feet, then

Camp, North Fork of the Merced

a sudden stop, and as sudden a start again; going all their journeys by quick, jerking impulses. These many stops I find are necessary as rests, for they are short-winded, and when pursued steadily are soon out of breath, pant pitifully, and are easily caught. Their bodies are more than half tail, but these tails are well managed, never heavily dragged nor curved up as if hard to carry; on the contrary, they seem to follow the body lightly of their own will. Some are colored like the sky, bright as bluebirds, others gray like the lichened rocks on which they hunt and bask.

Even the horned toad of the plains is a mild, harmless creature, and so are the snake-like species which glide in curves with true snake motion, while their small, undeveloped limbs drag as useless appendages. . . .

Mastodons and elephants used to live here no great geological time ago, as shown by their bones, often discovered by miners in washing gold-gravel. And bears of at least two species are here now, besides the California lion or panther, and wild cats, wolves, foxes, snakes, scorpions, wasps, tarantulas; but one is almost tempted at times to regard a small savage black ant as the master existence of this vast mountain world. These fearless, restless, wandering imps, though only about a quarter of an inch long, are fonder of fighting and biting than any beast I know. They attack every living thing around their homes, often without cause as far as I can see. Their bodies are mostly jaws curved like ice-hooks, and to get work for these weapons seems to be their chief aim and pleasure. Most of their colonies are established in living oaks somewhat decayed or hollowed, in which they can conveniently build their cells. These are chosen probably because of their strength as opposed to the attacks of animals and storms. They work both day and night, creep into dark caves, climb the highest trees, wander and hunt through cool ravines as well as on hot, unshaded ridges, and extend their highways and byways over everything but water and sky. From the foothills to a mile above the level of the sea nothing can stir without their knowledge; and alarms are spread in an incredibly short time, without any howl or cry that we can hear. I can't understand the need of their ferocious courage; there seems to be no common sense in it. Sometimes, no doubt, they fight in defense of their homes, but they fight anywhere and always wherever they can find anything to bite. As soon as a vulnerable spot is discovered on man or beast, they stand on their heads and sink their jaws, and though torn limb from limb, they will yet hold on and die biting deeper. When I contemplate this fierce creature so widely distributed and strongly intrenched, I see that much remains to be done ere the world is brought under the rule of universal peace and love.

On my way to camp a few minutes ago, I passed a dead pine nearly ten feet in diameter. It has been enveloped in fire from top to bottom so that now it looks like a grand black pillar set up as a monument. In this noble shaft a colony of large jet-black ants have established themselves, laboriously cutting tunnels and cells through the wood, whether sound or decayed. . . . Their towns are carved in fallen trunks as well as in those left standing, but never in sound, living trees or in the ground. When you happen to sit down to rest or take notes near a colony, some wandering hunter is sure to find you and come cautiously forward to discover the nature of the intruder and what ought to be done. If you are not too near the town and keep perfectly still he may run across your feet a few times, over your legs and hands and face, up your trousers, as if taking your measure and getting comprehensive views, then go in peace without raising an alarm. If, however, a tempting spot is offered or some suspicious movement excites him, a bite follows, and such a bite! I fancy that a bear or wolf bite is not to be compared with it. A quick electric flame of pain flashes along the outraged nerves, and you discover for the first time how great is the capacity for sensation you are possessed of. . . . Fortunately, if careful, one need not be bitten oftener than once or twice in a lifetime. This wonderful electric species is about three-fourths of an inch long. Bears are fond of them, and tear and gnaw their home-logs to pieces, and roughly devour the eggs, larvæ, parent ants, and the rotten or sound wood of the cells, all in one spicy acid hash. The Digger Indians also are fond of the larvæ and even of the perfect ants, so I have been told by old mountaineers. They bite off and reject the head, and eat the tickly acid body with keen relish. Thus are the poor biters bitten, like every other biter, big or little, in the world's great family. . . .

June 14

The pool-basins below the falls and cascades here-abouts, formed by the heavy down-plunging currents, are kept nicely clean and clear of detritus. The heavier parts of the material swept over the falls are heaped up a short distance in front of the basins in the form of a dam, thus tending, together with erosion, to increase their size. Sudden changes, however, are effected during the spring floods, when the snow is melting and the upper tributaries are roaring loud from "bank to brae." Then boulders that have fallen into the channels, and which the ordinary summer and winter currents were unable to move, are suddenly swept forward as by a mighty besom, hurled over the falls into these pools, and piled up in a new dam together with part of the old one, while some of the smaller boulders are carried farther down stream and variously lodged according to size and shape, all seeking rest where the force of the current is less than the resistance they are able to offer. But the greatest changes made in these relations of fall, pool, and dam are caused, not by the ordinary spring floods, but by extraordinary ones that occur at irregular intervals. The testimony of trees growing on flood boulder deposits shows that a century or more has passed since the last master flood came to awaken everything movable to go swirling and dancing on wonderful journeys. These floods may occur during the summer, when heavy thunder-showers, called "cloud-bursts," fall on wide, steeply inclined stream basins furrowed by converging channels, which suddenly gather the waters together into the main trunk in booming torrents of enormous transporting power, though short lived.

One of these ancient flood boulders stands firm in the middle of the stream channel, just below the lower edge of the pool dam at the foot of the fall nearest our camp. It is a nearly cubical mass of granite about eight feet high, plushed with mosses over the top and down the sides to ordinary high-water mark. When I climbed on top of it to-day and lay down to rest, it seemed the most romantic spot I had yet found—the one big stone with its mossy level top and smooth sides standing square and firm and solitary, like an altar, the fall in front of it bathing it lightly with the finest of the spray, just enough to keep its moss cover fresh; the clear green pool beneath, with its foam-bells and its half circle of lilies leaning forward like a band of admirers, and flowering dogwood and alder trees leaning over all in sun-sifted arches. How soothingly, restfully cool it is beneath that leafy, translucent ceiling, and how delightful the water music—the deep bass tones of the fall, the clashing, ringing spray, and infinite variety of small low tones of the current gliding past the side of the boulder-island, and glinting against a thousand smaller stones down the ferny channel! All this shut in; every one of these influences acting at short range as if in a quiet room. The place seemed holy, where one might hope to see God.

After dark, when the camp was at rest, I groped my way back to the altar boulder and passed the night on it,—above the water, beneath the leaves and stars,—everything still more impressive than by day, the fall seen dimly white, singing Nature's old love song with solemn enthusiasm, while the stars peering through the leaf-roof seemed to join in the white water's song. Precious night, precious day to abide in me forever. Thanks be to God for this immortal gift.

June 15

This noble tree [the sugar pine] is an inexhaustible study and source of pleasure. I never weary of gazing at its grand tassel cones, its perfectly round bole one hundred feet or more without a limb, the fine purplish color of its bark, and its magnificent outsweeping, down-curving feathery arms forming a crown always bold and striking and exhilarating. In habit and general port it looks somewhat like a palm, but no palm that I have yet seen

Sugar pine

displays such majesty of form and behavior either when poised silent and thoughtful in sunshine, or wide-awake waving in storm winds with every needle quivering. When young it is very straight and regular in form like most other conifers; but at the age of fifty to one hundred years it begins to acquire individuality, so that no two are alike in their prime or old age. Every tree calls for special admiration. I have been making many sketches, and regret that I cannot draw every needle. It is said to reach a height of three hundred feet, though the tallest I have measured falls short of this stature sixty feet or more. The diameter of the largest near the ground is about ten feet, though I've heard of some twelve feet thick or even fifteen. The diameter is held to a great height, the taper being almost imperceptibly gradual. Its companion, the yellow pine, is almost as large. The long silvery foliage of the younger specimens forms magnificent cylindrical brushes on the top shoots and the ends of the upturned branches, and when the wind sways the needles all one way at a certain angle every tree becomes a tower of white quivering sun-fire. Well may this shining species be called the silver pine.

The needles are sometimes more than a foot long, almost as long as those of the long-leaf pine of Florida. But though in size the yellow pine almost equals the sugar pine, and in rugged enduring strength seems to surpass it, it is far less marked in general habit and expression, with its regular conventional spire and its comparatively small cones clustered stiffly among the needles. Were there no sugar pine, then would this be the king of the world's eighty or ninety species, the brightest of the bright, waving, worshiping multitude. Were they mere mechanical sculptures, what noble objects they would still be! . . . the very gods of the plant kingdom, living their sublime century lives in sight of Heaven, watched and loved and admired from generation to generation! And how many other radiant resiny sun trees are here and higher up,—libocedrus, Douglas spruce, silver fir, sequoia. How rich our inheritance in these blessed mountains, the tree pastures into which our eyes are turned!

Now comes sundown. The west is all a glory of color transfiguring everything. Far up the Pilot Peak Ridge the radiant host of trees stand hushed and thoughtful, receiving the Sun's good-night, as solemn and impressive a leave-taking as if sun and trees were to meet no more. The daylight fades, the color spell is broken, and the forest breathes free in the night breeze beneath the stars.

June 16

One of the Indians from Brown's Flat got right into the middle of the camp this morning, unobserved. I was seated on a stone, looking over my notes and sketches, and happening to look up, was startled to see him standing grim and silent within a few steps of me, as motionless and weather-stained as an old tree-stump that had stood there for centuries. All Indians seem to have learned this wonderful way of walking unseen,—making themselves invisible like certain spiders I have been observing here, which, in case of alarm, caused, for example, by a bird alighting on the bush their webs are spread upon, immediately bounce themselves up and down on their elastic threads so rapidly that only a blur is visible. The wild Indian power of escaping observation, even where there is little or no cover to hide in, was probably slowly acquired in hard hunting and fighting lessons while trying to approach game, take enemies by surprise, or get safely away when compelled to retreat. And this experience transmitted through many generations seems at length to have become what is vaguely called instinct.

How smooth and changeless seems the surface of the mountains about us! Scarce a track is to be found beyond the range of the sheep except on small open spots on the sides of the streams, or where the forest carpets are thin or wanting. On the smoothest of these open strips and patches deer tracks may be seen, and the great suggestive footprints of bears, which, with those of the many small animals, are scarce enough to answer as a kind of light ornamental stitching or embroidery. Along the main ridges and larger branches of the river Indian trails may be traced, but they are not nearly as distinct as one would expect to find them. How many centuries Indians have roamed these woods nobody knows, probably a great many, extending far beyond the time that Columbus touched our shores, and it seems strange that heavier marks have not been made. Indians walk softly and hurt the landscape hardly more than the birds and squirrels, and their brush and bark huts last hardly longer than those of wood rats, while their more enduring monuments, excepting those wrought on the forests by the fires they made to improve their hunting grounds, vanish in a few centuries.

How different are most of those of the white man, especially on the lower gold region—roads blasted in the solid rock, wild streams dammed and tamed and turned out of their channels and led along the sides of canyons and valleys to work in mines like slaves. Crossing from ridge to ridge, high in the air, on long straddling trestles as if flowing on stilts, or down and up across valleys and hills, imprisoned in iron pipes to strike and wash away hills and miles of the skin of the mountain's face, riddling, stripping every gold gully and flat. These are the white man's marks made in a few feverish years, to say nothing of mills, fields, villages, scattered hundreds of miles along the flank of the Range. Long will it be ere these marks are effaced, though Nature is doing what she can, replanting, gardening, sweeping away old dams and flumes, leveling gravel and boulder piles, patiently trying to heal every raw scar. . . .

Sheep, like people, are ungovernable when hungry. Excepting my guarded lily gardens, almost every leaf that these hoofed locusts can reach within a radius of a mile or two from camp has been devoured. Even the bushes are stripped bare, and in spite of dogs and shepherds the sheep scatter to all points of the compass and vanish in dust. . . .

June 17

Counted the wool bundles this morning as they bounced through the narrow corral gate. About three hundred are missing, and as the shepherd could not go to seek them, I had to go. I tied a crust of bread to my belt, and with Carlo set out for the upper slopes of the Pilot Peak Ridge, and had a good day, notwithstanding the care of seeking the silly runaways. I went out for wool, and did not come back shorn. A peculiar light circled around the horizon, white and thin like that often seen over the auroral corona, blending into the blue of the upper sky. The only clouds were a few faint flossy pencilings like combed silk. I pushed direct to the boundary of the usual range of the flock, and around it until I found the outgoing trail of the wanderers. It led far up the ridge into an open place surrounded by a hedge-like growth of ceanothus chaparral. Carlo knew what I was about, and eagerly followed the scent until we came up to them, huddled in a timid, silent bunch. They had evidently been here all night and all the forenoon, afraid to go out to feed. Having escaped restraint, they were, like some people we know of, afraid of their freedom, did not know what to do with it, and seemed glad to get back into the old familiar bondage.

June 18

Another inspiring morning, nothing better in any world can be conceived. No description of Heaven that I have ever heard or read of seems half so fine. At noon the clouds occupied about .05 of the sky, white filmy touches drawn delicately on the azure.

The high ridges and hilltops beyond the woolly locusts are now gay with monardella, clarkia, coreopsis, and tall tufted grasses, some of them tall enough to wave like pines. The lupines, of which there are many ill-defined species, are now mostly out of flower, and many of the compositæ are beginning to fade, their radiant corollas vanishing in fluffy papus like stars in mist. . . .

June 19

    Pure sunshine all day. How beautiful a rock is made by leaf shadows! Those of the live oak are particularly clear and distinct, and beyond all art in grace and delicacy, now still as if painted on stone, now gliding softly as if afraid of noise, now dancing, waltzing in swift, merry swirls, or jumping on and off sunny rocks in quick dashes like wave embroidery on seashore cliffs. . . .

June 20

    . . . Who could ever guess that so rough a wilderness should yet be so fine, so full of good things. One seems to be in a majestic domed pavilion in which a grand play is being acted with scenery and music and incense,—all the furniture and action so interesting we are in no danger of being called on to endure one dull moment. . . .

Left camp early. Ran over the Tuolumne divide and down a few miles to a grove of sequoias that I had heard of, directed by the Don. They occupy an area of perhaps less than a hundred acres. Some of the trees are noble, colossal old giants, surrounded by magnificent sugar pines and Douglas spruces. The perfect specimens not burned or broken are singularly regular and symmetrical, though not at all conventional, showing infinite variety in general unity and harmony; the noble shafts with rich purplish brown fluted bark, free of limbs for one hundred and fifty feet or so, ornamented here and there with leafy rosettes; main branches of the oldest trees very large, crooked and rugged, zigzagging stiffly outward seemingly lawless, yet unexpectedly stooping just at the right distance from the trunk and dissolving in dense bossy masses of branchlets, thus making a regular though greatly varied outline,—a cylinder of leafy, outbulging spray masses, terminating in a noble dome, that may be recognized while yet far off upheaved against the sky above the dark bed of pines and firs and spruces, the king of all conifers, not only in size but in sublime majesty of behavior and port. I found a black, charred stump about thirty feet in diameter and eighty or ninety feet high—a venerable, impressive old monument of a tree that in its prime may have been the monarch of the grove; seedlings and saplings growing up here and there, thrifty and hopeful, giving no hint of the dying out of the species. Not any unfavorable change of climate, but only fire, threatens the existence of these noblest of God's trees.

". . . The trees round about them seem as perfect in beauty and form as the lilies, their boughs whorled like lily leaves in exact order. This evening . . . the glow of our campfire is working enchantment on everything within reach of its rays. Lying beneath the firs, it is glorious to see them dipping their spires in the starry sky, the sky like one vast lily meadow in bloom! How can I close my eyes on so precious a night."

June 23

Oh, these vast, calm, measureless mountain days, inciting at once to work and rest! Days in whose light everything seems equally divine, opening a thousand windows to show us God. Nevermore, however weary, should one faint by the way who gains the blessings of one mountain day; whatever his fate, long life, short life, stormy or calm, he is rich forever.

June 26

Nuttall's flowering dogwood makes a fine show when in bloom. The whole tree is then snowy white. The involucres are six to eight inches wide. Along the streams it is a good-sized tree thirty to fifty feet high, with a broad head when not crowded by companions. Its showy involucres attract a crowd of moths, butterflies, and other winged people about it for their own, and, I suppose, the tree's advantage. It likes plenty of cool water, and is a great drinker like the alder, wiilow, and cottonwood, and flourishes best on stream banks, though it often wanders far from streams in damp shady glens beneath the pines, where it is much smaller. When the leaves ripen in the fall, they become more beautiful than the flowers, displaying charming tones of red, purple, and lavender. . . .

June 24

Our regular allowance of clouds and thunder. Shepherd Billy is in a peck of trouble about the sheep; he declares that they are possessed with more of the evil one than any other flock from the beginning of the invention of mutton and wool to the last batch of it. No matter how many are missing, he will not, he says, go a step to seek them, because, as he reasons, while getting back one wanderer he would probably lose ten. Therefore runaway hunting must be Carlo's and mine. Billy's little dog Jack is also giving trouble by leaving camp every night to visit his neighbors up the mountain at Brown's Flat. He is a common-looking cur of no particular breed, but tremendously enterprising in love and war. He has cut all the ropes and leather straps he has been tied with, until his master in desperation, after climbing the brushy mountain again and again to drag him back, fastened him with a pole attached to his collar under his chin at one end, and to a stout sapling at the other. But the pole gave good leverage, and by constant twisting during the night, the fastening at the sapling end was chafed off, and he set out on his usual journey, dragging the pole through the brush, and reached the Indian settlement in safety. His master followed, and making no allowance, gave him a beating, and swore in bad terms that next evening he would "fix that infatuated pup" by anchoring him unmercifully to the heavy cast-iron lid of our Dutch oven, weighing about as much as the dog. It was linked directly to his collar close up under the chin, so that the poor fellow seemed unable to stir. He stood quite discouraged until after dark, unable to look about him, or even to lie down unless he stretched himself out with his front feet across the lid, and his head close down between his paws. Before morning, however, Jack was heard far up the height howling Excelsior, cast-iron anchor to the contrary notwithstanding. He must have walked, or rather climbed, erect on his hind legs, clasping the heavy lid like a shield against his breast, a formidable ironclad condition in which to meet his rivals. Next night, dog, pot-lid, and all, were tied up in an old beansack, and thus at last angry Billy gained the victory. Just before leaving home, Jack was bitten in the lower jaw by a rattlesnake, and for a week or so his head and neck were swollen to more than double the normal size; nevertheless he ran about as brisk and lively as ever, and is now completely recovered. The only treatment he got was fresh milk—a gallon or two at a time forcibly poured down his sore, poisoned throat.

June 29

I have been making the acquaintance of a very interesting little bird that flits about the falls and rapids of the main branches of the river. It is not a water-bird in structure, though it gets its living in the water, and never leaves the streams. It is not web-footed, yet it dives fearlessly into deep swirling rapids, evidently to feed at the bottom, using its wings to swim with under water just as ducks and loons do. Sometimes it wades about in shallow places, thrusting its head under from time to time in a jerking, nodding, frisky way that is sure to attract attention. It is about the size of a robin, has short crisp wings serviceable for flying either in water or air, and a tail of moderate size slanted upward, giving it, with its nodding, bobbing manners, a wrennish look. Its color is plain bluish ash, with a tinge of brown on the head and shoulders. It flies from fall to fall, rapid to rapid, with a solid whir of wing-beats like those of a quail, follows the windings of the stream, and usually alights on some rock jutting up out of the current, or on some stranded snag, or rarely on the dry limb of an overhanging tree, perching like regular tree birds when it suits its convenience. It has the oddest, daintiest mincing manners imaginable; and the little fellow can sing too, a sweet, thrushy, fluty song, rather low, not the least boisterous, and much less keen and accentuated than from its vigorous briskness one would be led to look for. . . . I have not yet found its nest, but it must be near the streams, for it never leaves them.

June 30

Half cloudy, half sunny, clouds lustrous white. The tall pines crowded along the top of the Pilot Peak Ridge look like six-inch miniatures exquisitely outlined on the satiny sky. Average cloudiness for the day about .25. No rain. And so this memorable month ends, a stream of beauty unmeasured, no more to be sectioned off by almanac arithmetic than sun-radiance or the currents of seas and rivers. . . .

"... The level bottom seemed to be dressed like a garden—sunny meadows here and there, and groves of pine and oak; the river ... flashing back the sunbeams."

On Through the Forest

July 1

. . . I like to watch the squirrels. There are two species here, the large California gray and the Douglas. The latter is the brightest of all the squirrels I have ever seen, a hot spark of life, making every tree tingle with his prickly toes, a condensed nugget of fresh mountain vigor and valor. . . . He seems to think the mountains belong to him, and at first tried to drive away the whole flock of sheep as well as the shepherd and dogs. How he scolds, and what faces he makes, all eyes, teeth, and whiskers! If not so comically small, he would indeed be a dreadful fellow. I should like to know more about his bringing up, his life in the home knot-hole, as well as in the treetops, throughout all seasons. Strange that I have not yet found a nest full of young ones. The Douglas is nearly allied to the red squirrel of the Atlantic slope, and may have been distributed to this side of the continent by way of the great unbroken forests of the north.

The California gray is one of the most beautiful, and, next to the Douglas, the most interesting of our hairy neighbors. Compared with the Douglas he is twice as large, but far less lively and influential as a worker in the woods and he manages to make his way through leaves and branches with less stir than his small brother. I have never heard him bark at anything except our dogs. When in search of food he glides silently from branch to branch, examining last year's cones, to see whether some few seeds may not be left between the scales, or gleans fallen ones among the leaves on the ground, since none of the present season's crop is yet available. His tail floats now behind him, now above him, level or gracefully curled like a wisp of cirrus cloud, every hair in its place, clean and shining and radiant as thistle-down in spite of rough, gummy work. His whole body seems about as unsubstantial as his tail. The little Douglas is fiery, peppery, full of brag and fight and show, with movements so quick and keen they almost sting the onlooker, and the harlequin gyrating show he makes of himself turns one giddy to see. The gray is shy, and oftentimes stealthy in his movements, as if half expecting an enemy in every tree and bush, and back of every log, wishing only to be let alone apparently, and

manifesting no desire to be seen or admired or feared. The Indians hunt this species for food, a good cause for caution, not to mention other enemies—hawks, snakes, wild cats. In woods where food is abundant they wear paths through sheltering thickets and over prostrate trees to some favorite pool where in hot and dry weather they drink at nearly the same hour every day. These pools are said to be narrowly watched, especially by the boys, who

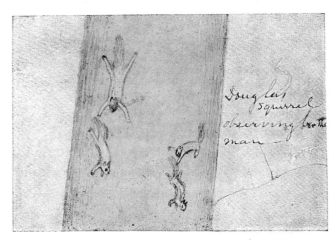

Douglas squirrel

lie in ambush with bow and arrow, and kill without noise. But, in spite of enemies, squirrels are happy fellows, forest favorites, types of tireless life. Of all Nature's wild beasts, they seem to me the wildest. May we come to know each other better.

The chaparral-covered hill-slope to the south of the camp . . . is the home and hiding-place of the curious wood rat (*Neotoma*), a handsome, interesting animal, always attracting attention wherever seen. It is more like a squirrel than a rat, is much larger, has delicate, thick, soft fur of a bluish slate color, white on the belly; ears large, thin, and translucent; eyes soft, full, and liquid; claws slender, sharp as needles; and as his limbs are strong, he can climb about as well as a squirrel. No rat or squirrel has so innocent a look, is so easily approached, or expresses such confidence in one's good intentions. He seems too fine for the thorny thickets he inhabits, and his hut also is as unlike himself as may be, though softly furnished inside. No other animal inhabitant of these mountains builds houses so large and striking in appearance. The traveler coming suddenly upon a group of them for the first time will not be likely to forget them. They are built of all kinds of sticks, old rotten pieces picked up anywhere, and green prickly twigs bitten from the nearest bushes, the whole mixed with miscellaneous odds and ends of everything movable, such as bits of cloddy earth, stones, bones, deerhorn, etc., piled up in a conical mass as if it were got ready for burning. Some of these curious cabins are six feet high and as wide at the base, and a dozen or more of them are occasionally grouped together, less perhaps for the sake of society than for advantages of food and shelter. . . .

July 2

. . . Pearl cumuli over the higher mountains—clouds, not with a silver lining, but all silver. The brightest, crispest, rockiest-looking clouds, most varied in features and keenest in outline I ever saw at any time of year in any country. The daily building and unbuilding of these snowy cloud-ranges—the highest Sierra—is a prime marvel to me, and I gaze at the stupendous white domes, miles high, with ever fresh admiration. But in the midst of these sky and mountain affairs a change of diet is pulling us down. We have been out of bread a few days, and begin to miss it more than seems reasonable, for we have plenty of meat and sugar and tea. Strange we should feel food-poor in so rich a wilderness. The Indians put us to shame, so do the squirrels,—starchy roots and seeds and bark in abundance, yet the failure of the meal sack disturbs our bodily balance, and threatens our best enjoyments.

July 4

. . . Mr. Delaney is expected to arrive soon from the lowlands with a new stock of provisions, and as the flock is to be moved to fresh pastures we shall all be well fed. In the mean time our stock of beans as well as flour has failed—everything but mutton, sugar, and tea. The shepherd is somewhat demoralized, and seems to care but little what becomes of his flock. He says that since the boss has failed to feed him he is not rightly bound to feed the sheep, and swears that no decent white man can climb these steep mountains on mutton alone. "It's not fittin' grub for a white man really white. For dogs and coyotes and Indians it's different. Good grub, good sheep. That's what I say." Such was Billy's Fourth of July oration.

July 6

Mr. Delaney has not arrived, and the bread famine is sore. We must eat mutton a while longer, though it seems hard to get accustomed to it. I have heard of Texas pio-

neers living without bread or anything made from the cereals for months without suffering, using the breast-meat of wild turkeys for bread. Of this kind they had plenty in the good old days when life, though considered less safe, was fussed over the less. The trappers and fur traders of early days in the Rocky Mountain regions lived on bison and beaver meat for months. Salmon-eaters, too, there are among both Indians and whites who seem to suffer little or not at all from the want of bread. Just at this moment mutton seems the least desirable of food, though of good quality. We pick out the leanest bits, and down they go against heavy disgust, causing nausea and an effort to reject the offensive stuff. Tea makes matters worse, if possible. The stomach begins to assert itself as an independent creature with a will of its own. We should boil lupine leaves, clover, starchy petioles, and saxifrage rootstocks like the Indians. We try to ignore our gastric troubles, rise and gaze about us, turn our eyes to the mountains, and climb doggedly up through brush and rocks into the heart of the scenery. A stifled calm comes on, and the day's duties and even enjoyments are languidly got through with. We chew a few leaves of ceanothus by way of luncheon, and smell or chew the spicy monardella for the dull headache and stomach-ache that now lightens, now comes muffling down upon us and into us like fog. At night more mutton, flesh to flesh, down with it, not too much, and there are the stars shining through the cedar plumes and branches above our beds.

July 7

. . . Bread without flesh is a good diet, as on many botanical excursions I have proved. Tea also may easily be ignored. Just bread and water and delightful toil is all I need,—not unreasonably much, yet one ought to be trained and tempered to enjoy life in these brave wilds in full independence of any particular kind of nourishment. That this may be accomplished is manifest, as far as bodily welfare is concerned, in the lives of people of other climes. The Eskimo, for example, gets a living far north of the wheat line, from oily seals and whales. Meat, berries, bitter weeds, and blubber, or only the last, for months at a time; and yet these people all around the frozen shores of our continent are said to be hearty, jolly, stout, and brave. We hear, too, of fish-eaters, carnivorous as spiders, yet well enough as far as stomachs are concerned, while we are so ridiculously helpless, making wry faces over our fare, looking sheepish in digestive distress amid rumbling, grumbling sounds that might well pass for smothered baas. We have a large supply of sugar, and this evening it occured to me that these belligerent stomachs might possibly, like complaining children, be coaxed with candy. Accordingly the frying-pan was cleansed, and a lot of sugar cooked in it to a sort of wax, but this stuff only made matters worse.

Man seems to be the only animal whose food soils him, making necessary much washing and shield-like bibs and napkins. Moles living in the earth and eating slimy worms are yet as clean as seals or fishes, whose lives are one perpetual wash. And, as we have seen, the squirrels in these resiny woods keep themselves clean in some mysterious way; not a hair is sticky, though they handle the gummy cones, and glide about apparently without care. The birds, too, are clean, though they seem to make a good deal of fuss washing and cleaning their feathers. Certain flies and ants I see are in a fix, entangled and sealed up in the sugar-wax we threw away, like some of their ancestors in amber. Our stomachs, like tired muscles, are sore with long squirming. Once I was very hungry in the Bonaventure graveyard near Savannah, Georgia, having fasted for several days; then the empty stomach seemed to chafe in much the same way as now, and a somewhat similar tenderness and aching was produced, hard to bear, though the pain was not acute. We dream of bread, a sure sign we need it. Like the Indians, we ought to know how to get the starch out of fern and saxifrage stalks, lily bulbs, pine bark, etc. Our education has been sadly neglected for many generations. Wild rice would be good. I noticed a leersia in wet meadow edges, but the seeds are small. Acorns are not ripe, nor pine nuts, nor filberts. The inner bark of pine or spruce might be tried. Drank tea until half intoxicated. Man seems to crave a stimulant when anything extraordinary is going on, and this is the only one I use. Billy chews great quantities of tobacco, which I suppose helps to stupefy and moderate his misery. We look and listen for the Don every hour. How beautiful upon the mountains his big feet would be!

In the warm, hospitable Sierra, shepherds and mountain men in general, as far as I have seen, are easily satisfied as to food supplies and bedding. Most of them are heartily content to "rough it," ignoring Nature's fineness as bothersome or unmanly. The shepherd's bed is often only the bare ground and a pair of blankets, with a stone, a piece of wood, or a packsaddle for a pillow. In choosing the spot, he shows less care than the dogs, for they usually deliberate before making up their minds in so important an affair, going from place to place, scraping away loose sticks and pebbles, and trying for comfort by making many changes, while the shepherd casts himself down anywhere, seemingly the least skilled of all rest seekers. His food, too, even when he has all he wants, is usually far from delicate, either in kind or cooking. Beans, bread of any sort, bacon, mutton, dried peaches, and sometimes potatoes and onions, make up his bill-of-fare, the two latter articles being regarded as luxuries on account of their weight as compared with the nourishment they contain; a half-sack or so of each may be put into the pack in setting out from the home ranch and in a few days they are done. Beans are the main standby, portable, wholesome, and capable of going far, besides being easily cooked, although curiously enough a great deal of mystery is supposed to lie about the bean-pot. No two cooks quite agree on the methods of making beans do their best, and, after petting and coaxing and nursing the savory mess, —well oiled and mellowed with bacon boiled into the heart of it,—the proud cook will ask, after dishing out a quart or two for trial, "Well, how do you like *my* beans?" as if by no possibility could they be like any other beans cooked in the same way, but must needs possess some special virtue of which he alone is master. Molasses, sugar, or pepper may be used to give desired flavors; or the first water may be poured off and a spoonful or two of ashes or soda added to dissolve or soften the skins more fully, according to various tastes and notions. But, like casks of wine, no two potfuls are exactly alike to every palate. Some are supposed to be spoiled by the moon, by some unlucky day, by the beans having been grown on soil not suitable; or the whole year may be to blame as not favorable for beans.

Coffee, too, has it marvels in the camp kitchen, but not so many, and not so inscrutable as those that beset the bean-pot. A low, complacent grunt follows a mouthful drawn in with a gurgle, and the remark cast forth aimlessly, "That's good coffee." Then another gurgling sip and repetition of the judgment, "*Yes, sir, that is good coffee.*" As to tea, there are but two kinds, weak and strong, the stronger the better. The only remark heard is, "That tea's weak," otherwise it is good enough and not worth mentioning. If it has been boiled an hour or two or smoked on a pitchy fire, no matter,—who cares for a little tannin or creosote? they make the black beverage all the stronger and more attractive to tobacco-tanned palates.

. . . At last Don Delaney comes . . . hunger vanishes, we turn our eyes to the mountains, and to-morrow we go climbing toward cloudland.

Never while anything is left of me shall this first camp be forgotten. It has fairly grown into me, not merely as memory pictures, but as part and parcel of mind and body alike. . . .

July 8

Now away we go toward the topmost mountains. . . .

Up through the woods the hoofed locusts streamed beneath a cloud of brown dust. Scarcely were they driven a hundred yards from the old corral ere they seemed to know that at last they were going to new pastures, and rushed wildly ahead, crowding through gaps in the brush, jumping, tumbling like exulting hurrahing flood-waters escaping through a broken dam. A man on each flank kept shouting advice to the leaders, who in their famishing condition were behaving like Gadarene swine; two other drivers were busy with stragglers, helping them out of brush tangles; the Indian, calm, alert, silently watched for wanderers likely to be overlooked; the two dogs ran here and there, at a loss to know what was best to be done, while the Don, soon far in the rear, was trying to keep in sight of his troublesome wealth.

As soon as the boundary of the old eaten-out range was passed the hungry horde suddenly became calm, like a mountain stream in a meadow. Thenceforward they were allowed to eat their way as slowly as they wished, care being taken only to keep them headed toward the summit of the Merced and Tuolumne divide. Soon the two thousand flattened paunches were bulged out with sweetpea vines and grass, and the gaunt, desperate creatures, more like wolves than sheep, became bland and governable, while the howling drivers changed to gentle shepherds, and sauntered in peace.

Toward sundown we reached Hazel Green . . . on the summit of the dividing ridge between the basins of the Merced and Tuolumne, where there is a small brook flowing through hazel and dogwood thickets beneath magnificent silver firs and pines. Here, we are camped for the night, our big fire heaped high with rosiny logs and branches. . . .

We have now reached a height of six thousand feet. In the forenoon we passed along a flat part of the dividing ridge that is planted with manzanita (*Arctostaphylos*), some specimens the largest I have seen. I measured one, the bole of which is four feet in diameter and only eighteen inches high from the ground, where it dissolves into many widespreading branches forming a broad round head about ten or twelve feet high, covered with clusters of small narrow-throated pink bells. . . . I wonder how old these curious tree-bushes are, probably as old as the great pines. Indians and bears and birds and fat grubs feast on the berries, which look like small apples, often rosy on one side, green on the other. The Indians are said to make a kind of beer or cider out of them. There are many species. This one, *Arctostaphylos pungens,* is common hereabouts. No need

have they to fear the wind, so low they are and steadfastly rooted. Even the fires that sweep the woods seldom destroy them utterly, for they rise again from the root, and some of the dry ridges they grow on are seldom touched by fire. . . .

July 9

Exhilarated with the mountain air, I feel like shouting this morning with excess of wild animal joy. The Indian lay down away from the fire last night, without blankets,

Divide between the Tuolumne and the Merced, below Hazel Green

having nothing on, by way of clothing, but a pair of blue overalls and a calico shirt wet with sweat. The night air is chilly at this elevation, and we gave him some horse-blankets, but he didn't seem to care for them. A fine thing to be independent of clothing where it is so hard to carry. When food is scarce, he can live on whatever comes in his way—a few berries, roots, bird eggs, grasshoppers, black ants, fat wasp or bumblebee larvæ, without feeling that he is doing anything worth mention, so I have been told.

Our course to-day was along the broad top of the main ridge to a hollow beyond Crane Flat. It is scarce at all rocky, and is covered with the noblest pines and spruces I have yet seen. Sugar pines from six to eight feet in diameter are not uncommon, with a height of two hundred feet or even more. The silver firs (*Abies concolor* and *A. magnifica*) are exceedingly beautiful, especially the *magnifica,* which becomes more abundant the higher we go. It is of great size, one of the most notable in every way of the giant conifers of the Sierra. I saw specimens that measured seven feet in diameter and over two hundred feet in height. . . .

At Crane Flat we climbed a thousand feet or more in a distance of about two miles, the forest growing more dense and the silvery *magnifica* fir forming a still greater portion of the whole. Crane Flat is a meadow with a wide sandy border lying on the top of the divide. It is often visited by blue cranes to rest and feed on their long journeys, hence the name. It is about half a mile long, draining into the Merced, sedgy in the middle, with a margin bright with lilies, columbines, larkspurs, lupines, castilleia, then an outer zone of dry, gently sloping ground starred with a multitude of small flowers. . . .

. . . But the glory of these forest meadows is a lily (*L. parvum*). The tallest are from seven to eight feet high with magnificent racemes of ten to twenty or more small orange-colored flowers. . . . It varies, I find, very much in size even in the same meadow, not only with the soil, but with age. I saw a specimen that had only one flower, and another within a stone's throw had twenty-five. And to think that the sheep should be allowed in these lily meadows! after how many centuries of Nature's care planting and watering them, tucking the bulbs in snugly below winter frost, shading the tender shoots with clouds drawn above them like curtains, pouring refreshing rain, making them perfect in beauty, and keeping them safe by a thousand miracles; yet, strange to say, allowing the trampling of devastating sheep. One might reasonably look for a wall of fire to fence such gardens. So extravagent is Nature with her choicest treasures, spending plant beauty as she spends sunshine, pouring it forth into land and sea, garden and desert. And so the beauty of lilies falls on angels and men, bears and squirrels, wolves and sheep, . . . but as far as I have seen, man alone, and the animals he tames, destroy these gardens. Awkward, lumbering bears, the Don tells me, love to wallow in them in hot weather, and deer with their sharp feet cross them again and again, sauntering and feeding, yet never a lily have I seen spoiled by them. Rather, like gardeners, they seem to cultivate them, pressing and dibbling as required. Anyhow not a leaf or petal seems misplaced.

The trees round about them seem as perfect in beauty and form as the lilies, their boughs whorled like lily leaves in exact order. This evening, as usual, the glow of our campfire is working enchantment on everything within reach of its rays. Lying beneath the firs, it is glorious to see them dipping their spires in the starry sky, the sky like one vast lily meadow in bloom! How can I close my eyes on so precious a night?

July 10

. . . On through the forest ever higher we go, a cloud of dust dimming the way, thousands of feet trampling leaves and flowers. . . . They cannot hurt the trees, though some of the seedlings suffer, and should the woolly locusts be greatly multiplied, as on account of dollar value they are likely to be, then the forests, too, may in time be destroyed. Only the sky will then be safe, though hid from view by dust and smoke, incense of a bad sacrifice. Poor, helpless, hungry sheep, in great part misbegotten, without good right to be, semi-manufactured, made less by God than man, born out of time and place, yet their voices are strangely human and call out one's pity. . . .

Fortunately the sheep need little attention, as they are driven slowly and allowed to nip and nibble as they like. Since leaving Hazel Green we have been following the Yosemite trail; visitors to the famous valley coming by way of Coulterville and Chinese Camp pass this way— the two trails uniting at Crane Flat—and enter the valley on the north side. Another trail enters on the south side by way of Mariposa. The tourists we saw were in parties of from three or four to fifteen or twenty, mounted on mules or small mustang ponies. A strange show they made, winding single file through the solemn woods in gaudy attire, scaring the wild creatures, and one might fancy that even the great pines would be disturbed and groan aghast. But what may we say of ourselves and the flock?

We are now camped at Tamarack Flat, within four or five miles of the lower end of Yosemite. Here is another fine meadow embosomed in the woods, with a deep, clear stream gliding through it, its banks rounded and beveled with a thatch of dipping sedges. The flat is named after the two-leaved pine (*Pinus contorta,* var. *Murrayana*), common here, especially around the cool margin of the meadow. On rocky ground it is a rough, thickset tree, about forty to sixty feet high and one to three feet in diameter, bark thin and gummy, branches rather naked, tassels, leaves, and cones small. But in damp, rich soil it grows close and slender, and reaches a height at times of nearly a hundred feet. Specimens only six inches in diameter at the ground are often fifty or sixty feet in height, as slender and sharp in outline as arrows, like the true tamarack (larch) of the Eastern States; hence the name, though it is a pine.

July 11

The Don has gone ahead on one of the pack animals to spy out the land to the north of Yosemite in search of the best point for a central camp. Much higher than this we cannot now go, for the upper pastures, said to be better than any hereabouts, are still buried in heavy winter snow. Glad I am that camp is to be fixed in the Yosemite region. . . .

We are now about seven thousand feet above the sea, and the nights are so cool we have to pile coats and extra clothing on top of our blankets. Tamarack Creek is icy cold, delicious, exhilarating champagne water. It is flowing bank-full in the meadow with silent speed, but only a few hundred yards below our camp the ground is bare gray granite strewn with boulders, large spaces being without a single tree or only a small one here and there anchored in narrow seams and cracks. The boulders, many of them very large, are not in piles or scattered like rubbish among loose crumbling debris as if weathered out of the solid as boulders of disintegration; they mostly occur singly, and are lying on a clean pavement on which the sunshine falls in a glare that contrasts with the shimmer of light and shade we have been accustomed to in the leafy woods. And, strange to say, these boulders lying so still and deserted, with no moving force near them, no boulder carrier anywhere in sight, were nevertheless brought from a distance, as difference in color and composition shows, quarried and carried and laid down here each in its place; nor have they stirred, most of them, through calm and storm since first they arrived. They look lonely here, strangers in a strange land,—huge blocks, angular mountain chips, the largest twenty or thirty feet in diameter, the chips that Nature has made in modeling her landscapes, fashioning the forms of her mountains and valleys. And with what tool were they quarried and carried? On the pavement we find its marks. The most resisting unweathered portion of the surface is scored and striated in a rigidly parallel way, indicating that the region has been overswept by a glacier from the northeastward, grinding down the general mass of the mountains, scoring and polishing, producing a strange, raw, wiped appearance, and dropping whatever boulders it chanced to be carrying at the time it was melted at the close of the Glacial Period. A fine discovery this. As for the forests we have been passing through, they are probably growing on deposits of soil most of which has been laid down by this same ice agent in the form of moraines of different sorts, now in great part disintegrated and outspread by post-glacial weathering.

Out of the grassy meadow and down over this ice-planed granite runs the glad young Tamarack Creek, . . . and cascades on its way to the Merced Canyon, a few miles below Yosemite, falling more than three thousand feet in a distance of about two miles.

All the Merced streams are wonderful singers, and Yosemite is the center where the main tributaries meet. From a point about half a mile from our camp we can see into the lower end of the famous valley, with its wonderful cliffs and groves, a grand page of mountain manuscript that I would gladly give my life to be able to read. How vast it seems, how short human life when we happen to think of it, and how little we may learn, however hard we try! Yet why bewail our poor inevitable ignorance?

Some of the external beauty is always in sight, enough to keep every fibre of us tingling, and this we are able to gloriously enjoy though the methods of its creation may lie beyond our ken. . . .

Have greatly enjoyed all this huge day, sauntering and seeing, steeping in the mountain influences, sketching, noting, pressing flowers, drinking ozone and Tamarack water. . . .

A log house serves to mark a claim to the Tamarack meadow, which may become valuable as a station in case travel to Yosemite should greatly increase. Belated parties occasionally stop here. A white man with an Indian woman is holding possession of the place. . . .

July 12

The Don has returned, and again we go on pilgrimage. "Looking over the Yosemite Creek country," he said, "from the tops of the hills you see nothing but rocks and patches of trees; but when you go down into the rocky desert you find no end of small grassy banks and meadows, and so the country is not half so lean as it looks. There we'll go and stay until the snow is melted from the upper country."

I was glad to hear that the high snow made a stay in the Yosemite region necessary, for I am anxious to see as much of it as possible. What fine times I shall have sketching, studying plants and rocks, and scrambling about the brink of the great valley alone, out of sight and sound of camp!

We saw another party of Yosemite tourists to-day. Somehow most of these travelers seem to care but little for the glorious objects about them, though enough to spend time and money and endure long rides to see the famous valley. . . .

We moved slowly eastward along the Mono Trail, and early in the afternoon unpacked and camped on the bank of Cascade Creek. . . .

. . . Never was stream more fittingly named, for as far as I have traced it above and below our camp it is one continuous bouncing, dancing, white bloom of cascades. And at the very last unwearied it finishes its wild course in a grand leap of three hundred feet or more to the bottom of the main Yosemite Canyon. . . . Here I find the little water ouzel . . . seeming to take the greater delight the more boisterous the stream. The dizzy precipices, the swift dashing energy displayed, and the thunder tones of the sheer falls are awe-inspiring, but there is nothing awful about this little bird. Its song is sweet and low, and all its gestures, as it flits about amid the loud uproar, bespeak strength and peace. . . . A yet finer bloom is this little bird than the foam-bells in eddying pools. . . .

". . . Drinking this champagne water is pure pleasure, so is breathing the living air, and every movement of limbs is pleasure, while the whole body seems to feel beauty when exposed to it as it feels the campfire or sunshine, entering not by the eyes alone . . . One's body then seems homogeneous throughout, sound as a crystal."

June 13

"Another glorious Sierra day in which one seems to be dissolved and absorbed and sent pulsing onward we know not where. Life seems neither long nor short, and we take no more heed to save time or make haste than do the trees and stars. This is true freedom, a good practical sort of immortality. . . ."

"... And how soft and lovely the light streaming through this living ceiling, revealing the arching branching ribs and veins of the fronds as the framework of countless panes of pale green and yellow plant-glass nicely fitted together—a fairyland created out of the commonest fernstuff."

"Walk the Sequoia woods at any time of the year and you will say they are the most beautiful and majestic on earth. Beautiful and impressive contrasts meet you everywhere the colors of tree and flower, rock and sky, light and shade, strength and frailty, endurance and evanescence . . ."

July 13

Our course all day has been eastward over the rim of Yosemite Creek basin and down about halfway to the bottom, where we have encamped on a sheet of glacier-polished granite, a firm foundation for beds. Saw the tracks of a very large bear on the trail, and the Don talked of bears in general. . . . Lambs, the Don told me, born in the lowland, that never saw or heard a bear, snort and run in terror when they catch the scent, showing how fully they have inherited a knowledge of their enemy. Hogs, mules, horses, and cattle are afraid of bears, and are seized with ungovernable terror when they approach, particularly hogs and mules. Hogs are frequently driven to pastures in the foothills of the Coast Range and Sierra where acorns are abundant, and are herded in droves of hundreds like sheep. When a bear comes to the range they promptly leave it, emigrating in a body, usually in the night time, the keepers being powerless to prevent; they thus show more sense than sheep, that simply scatter in the rocks and brush and await their fate. Mules flee like the wind with or without riders when they see a bear, and, if picketed, sometimes break their necks in trying to break their ropes, though I have not heard of bears killing mules or horses. . . .

Night is coming on, the gray rock waves are growing dim in the twilight. How raw and young this region appears! Had the ice sheet that swept over it vanished but yesterday, its traces on the more resisting portions about our camp could hardly be more distinct than they now are. The horses and sheep and all of us, indeed, slipped on the smoothest places.

July 14

. . . In an hour or two we came to Yosemite Creek, the stream that makes the greatest of all the Yosemite falls. It is about forty feet wide at the Mono Trail crossing, and now about four feet in average depth, flowing about three miles an hour. The distance to the verge of the Yosemite wall, where it makes its tremendous plunge, is only about two miles from here. Calm, beautiful, and nearly silent, it glides with stately gestures, a dense growth of the slender two-leaved pine along its banks, and a fringe of willow, purple spirea, sedges, daisies, lilies, and columbines. Some of the sedges and willow boughs dip into the current, and just outside of the close ranks of trees there is a sunny flat of washed gravelly sand which seems to have been deposited by some ancient flood. . . . Back of this flowery strip there is a wavy unsloping plain of solid granite, so smoothly ice-polished in many places that it glistens in the sun like glass. In shallow hollows there are patches of

trees, mostly the rough form of the two-leaved pine, rather scrawny looking where there is little or no soil. Also a few junipers (*Juniperus occidentalis*), short and stout, with bright cinnamon-colored bark and gray foliage, standing alone mostly, on the sun-beaten pavement, safe from fire, clinging by slight joints,—a sturdy storm-enduring mountaineer of a tree, living on sunshine and snow, maintaining tough health on this diet for perhaps more than a thousand years.

Junipers in Tenaya Canyon

Up towards the head of the basin I see groups of domes rising above the wavelike ridges, and some picturesque castellated masses, and dark strips and patches of silver fir, indicating deposits of fertile soil. Would that I could command the time to study them! What rich excursions one could make in this well-defined basin! Its glacial inscriptions and sculptures, how marvelous they seem, how noble the studies they offer! . . .

The drivers and dogs had a lively, laborious time getting the sheep across the creek, the second large stream thus far that they have been compelled to cross without a bridge; the first being the North Fork of the Merced near Bower Cave. Men and dogs, shouting and barking, drove the timid, water-fearing creatures in a close crowd against the bank, but not one of the flock would launch away. While thus jammed, the Don and the shepherd rushed through the frightened crowd to stampede those in front, but this would only cause a break backward, and away they would scamper through the stream-bank trees and scatter over the rocky pavement. Then with the aid of the dogs the runaways would again be gathered and made to face the stream, and again the compacted mass would break away, amid wild shouting and barking that might well have disturbed the stream itself and marred the music of its falls, to which visitors no doubt from all quarters of the globe were listening. "Hold them there! Now hold them there!" shouted the Don; "the front ranks will soon tire of the pressure, and be glad to take to the water, then all will jump in and cross in a hurry." But they did nothing of the kind; they only avoided the pressure by breaking back in scores and hundreds, leaving the beauty of the banks sadly trampled.

If only one could be got to cross over, all would make haste to follow; but that one could not be found. A lamb was caught, carried across, and tied to a bush on the opposite bank, where it cried piteously for its mother. But though greatly concerned, the mother only called it back. That play on maternal affection failed, and we began to fear that we should be forced to make a long roundabout drive and cross the wide-spread tributaries of the creek in succession. This would require several days, but it had its advantages, for I was eager to see the sources of so famous a stream. Don Quixote, however, determined that they must ford just here, and immediately began a sort of siege by cutting down slender pines on the bank and building a corral barely large enough to hold the flock when well pressed together. And as the stream would form one side of the corral he believed that they could easily be forced into the water.

In a few hours the inclosure was completed, and the silly animals were driven in and rammed hard against the brink of the ford. Then the Don, forcing a way through the compacted mass, pitched a few of the terrified unfortunates into the stream by main strength; but instead of crossing over, they swam about close to the bank, making desperate attempts to get back into the flock. Then a dozen or more were shoved off, and the Don, tall like a crane and a good natural wader, jumped in after them, seized a struggling wether, and dragged it to the opposite shore. But no sooner did he let it go than it jumped into the stream and swam back to its frightened companions in the corral, thus manifesting sheep-nature as unchange-

able as gravitation. Pan with his pipes would have had no better luck, I fear. We were now pretty well baffled. The silly creatures would suffer any sort of death rather than cross that stream. Calling a council, the dripping Don declared that starvation was now the only likely scheme to try, and that we might as well camp here in comfort and let the besieged flock grow hungry and cool, and come to their senses, if they had any. In a few minutes after being thus let alone, an adventurer in the foremost rank plunged in and swam bravely to the farther shore. Then suddenly all rushed in pell-mell together, trampling one another under water, while we vainly tried to hold them back. The Don jumped into the thickest of the gasping, gurgling, drowning mass, and shoved them right and left as if each sheep was a piece of floating timber. The current also served to drift them apart; a long bent column was soon formed, and in a few minutes all were over and began baaing and feeding as if nothing out of the common had happened. That none were drowned seems wonderful. I fully expected that hundreds would gain the romantic fate of being swept into Yosemite over the highest waterfall in the world.

As the day was far spent, we camped a little way back from the ford, and let the dripping flock scatter and feed until sundown. The wool is dry now, and calm, cud-chewing peace has fallen on all the comfortable band, leaving no trace of the watery battle. I have seen fish driven out of the water with less ado than was made in driving these animals into it. Sheep brain must surely be poor stuff. Compare to-day's exhibition with the performances of deer swimming quietly across broad and rapid rivers, and from island to island in seas and lakes; or with dogs, or even with the squirrels that, as the story goes, cross the Mississippi River on selected chips, with tails for sails comfortably trimmed to the breeze. A sheep can hardly be called an animal; an entire flock is required to make one foolish individual.

The Yosemite

Followed the Mono Trail up the eastern rim of the basin nearly to its summit, then turned off southward to a small shallow valley that extends to the edge of the Yosemite, which we reached about noon, and encamped. After luncheon I made haste to high ground, and from the top of the ridge on the west side of Indian Canyon gained the noblest view of the summit peaks I have ever yet enjoyed. Nearly all the upper basin of the Merced was displayed . . . domes and canyons, dark upsweeping forests, and glorious array of white peaks deep in the sky. . . .

Following the ridge, which made a gradual descent to the south, I came at length to the brow of that massive cliff that stands between Indian Canyon and Yosemite Falls, and here the far-famed valley came suddenly into view throughout almost its whole extent. The noble walls—sculptured into endless variety of domes and gables, spires and battlements and plain mural precipices—all a-tremble with the thunder tones of the falling water. The level bottom seemed to be dressed like a garden—sunny meadows here and there, and groves of pine and oak; the river of Mercy sweeping in majesty through the midst of them and flashing back the sunbeams. The great Tissiack, or Half-Dome, rising at the upper end of the valley to a height of nearly a mile, is nobly proportioned and life-like, the most impressive of all the rocks, holding the eye in devout admiration, calling it back again and again from falls or meadows, or even the mountains beyond,—marvelous cliffs, marvelous in sheer dizzy depth and sculpture, types of endurance. Thousands of years have they stood in the sky exposed to rain, snow, frost, earthquake and avalanche, yet they still wear the bloom of youth.

I rambled along the valley rim to the westward; most of it is rounded off on the very brink, so that it is not easy to find places where one may look clear down the face of the wall to the bottom. When such places were found, and I had cautiously set my feet and drawn my body erect, I could not help fearing a little that the rock might split off and let me down, and what a down!—more than three thousand feet. Still my limbs did not tremble, nor did I feel the least uncertainty as to the reliance to be placed on them. My only fear was that a flake of the granite, which in some places showed joints more or less open and running parallel with the face of the cliff, might give way. After withdrawing from such places, excited with the view I had got, I would say to myself, "Now don't go out on the verge again." But in the face of Yosemite scenery cautious remonstrance is vain; under its spell one's body seems to go where it likes with a will over which we seem to have scarce any control.

After a mile or so of this memorable cliff work I approached Yosemite Creek, admiring its easy, graceful, confident gestures as it comes bravely forward in its narrow channel, singing the last of its mountain songs on its way to its fate—a few rods more over the shining granite, then down half a mile in showy foam to another world, to be lost in the Merced, where climate, vegetation, inhabitants, all are different. Emerging from its last gorge, it glides in wide lace-like rapids down a smooth incline into a pool where it seems to rest and compose its gray, agitated waters before taking the grand plunge, then slowly slipping over the lip of the pool basin, it descends another glossy slope with rapidly accelerated speed to the brink of the tremendous cliff, and with sublime, fateful confidence springs out free in the air.

I took off my shoes and stockings and worked my way cautiously down alongside the rushing flood, keeping my feet and hands pressed firmly on the polished rock. The booming, roaring water, rushing past close to my head, was very exciting. I had expected that the sloping apron would terminate with the perpendicular wall of the valley, and that from the foot of it, where it is less steeply inclined, I should be able to lean far enough out to see the forms and behavior of the fall all the way down to the bottom. But I found that there was yet another small brow over which I could not see, and which appeared to be too steep for mortal feet. Scanning it keenly, I discovered a narrow shelf about three inches wide on the very brink, just wide enough for a rest for one's heels. But there seemed to be no way of reaching it over so steep a brow. At length, after careful scrutiny of the surface, I found an irregular edge of a flake of the rock some distance back from the margin of the torrent. If I was to get down to the brink at all, that rough edge, which might offer slight finger-holds, was the only way. But the slope beside it looked dangerously smooth and steep, and the swift roaring flood beneath, overhead, and beside me was very nerve-trying. I therefore concluded not to venture farther, but did nevertheless. Tufts of artemisia were growing in clefts of the rock near by, and I filled my mouth with the bitter leaves, hoping they might help to prevent giddiness. Then, with a caution not known in ordinary circumstances, I crept down safely to the little ledge, got my heels well planted on it, then shuffled in a horizontal direction twenty or thirty feet until close to the outplunging current, which, by the time it had descended thus far, was already white. Here I obtained a perfectly free view down into the heart of the snowy, chanting throng of comet-like streamers, into which the body of the fall soon separates.

While perched on that narrow niche I was not distinctly conscious of danger. The tremendous grandeur of the fall in form and sound and motion, acting at close range, smothered the sense of fear, and in such places one's body takes keen care for safety on its own account. How long I remained down there, or how I returned, I can hardly tell. Anyhow I had a glorious time, and got back to camp about dark, enjoying triumphant exhilaration soon followed by dull weariness. . . .

July 16

My enjoyments yesterday afternoon, especially at the head of the fall, were too great for good sleep. Kept starting up last night in a nervous tremor, half awake, fancying that the foundation of the mountain we were camped on had given way and was falling into Yosemite Valley. In vain I roused myself to make a new beginning for sound sleep. The nerve strain had been too great, and again and again I dreamed I was rushing through the air above a glorious avalanche of water and rocks. . . .

Left camp soon after sunrise for an all-day ramble eastward. Crossed the head of Indian Basin, forested with *Abies magnifica*, underbrush mostly *Ceanothus cordulatus* and manzanita, a mixture not easily trampled over or penetrated, for the ceanothus is thorny and grows in dense snow-pressed masses, and the manzanita has exceedingly crooked, stubborn branches. From the head of the canyon continued on past North Dome into the basin of Dome

or Porcupine Creek. . . . Had more magnificent views of the upper mountains, and of the great South Dome, said to be the grandest rock in the world. Well it may be, since it is of such noble dimensions and sculpture. A wonderfully impressive monument, its lines exquisite in fineness, and though sublime in size, is finished like the finest work of art, and seems to be alive. . . .

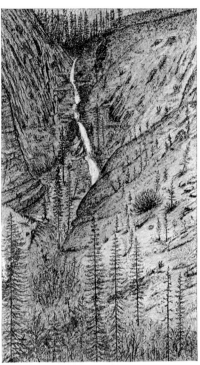

Approach of Dome Creek to Yosemite

July 18

Slept pretty well; the valley walls did not seem to fall, though I still fancied myself at the brink, alongside the white, plunging flood, especially when half asleep. Strange the danger of that adventure should be more troublesome now that I am in the bosom of the peaceful woods, a mile or more from the fall, than it was while I was on the brink of it.

Bears seem to be common here, judging by their tracks. About noon we had another rainstorm with keen startling thunder, the metallic, ringing, clashing, clanging notes gradually fading into low bass rolling and muttering in the distance. For a few minutes the rain came in a grand torrent like a waterfall, then hail; some of the hailstones an inch in diameter, hard, icy, and irregular in form, like those oftentimes seen in Wisconsin. Carlo watched them with intelligent astonishment as they came pelting and thrashing through the quivering branches of the trees. . . .

July 19

Watching the daybreak and sunrise. The pale rose and purple sky changing softly to daffodil yellow and white, sunbeams pouring through the passes between the peaks and over the Yosemite domes, making their edges burn; the silver firs in the middle ground catching the glow on their spiry tops. . . .

About noon, as usual, big bossy cumuli began to grow above the forest, and the rainstorm pouring from them is the most imposing I have yet seen. The silvery zigzag lightning lances are longer than usual, and the thunder gloriously impressive, keen, crashing, intensely concentrated, speaking with such tremendous energy it would seem that an entire mountain is being shattered at every stroke, but probably only a few trees are being shattered, many of which I have seen on my walks hereabouts strewing the ground. At last the clear ringing strokes are succeeded by deep low tones that grow gradually fainter as they roll afar into the recesses of the echoing mountains, where they seem to be welcomed home. Then another and another peal, or rather crashing, splintering stroke, follows in quick succession, perchance splitting some giant pine or fir from top to bottom into long rails and slivers, and scattering them to all points of the compass. Now comes the rain, with corresponding extravagant grandeur, covering the ground high and low with a sheet of flowing water, a transparent film fitted like a skin upon the rugged anatomy of the landscape, making the rocks glitter and glow, gathering in the ravines, flooding the streams, and making them shout and boom in reply to the thunder.

How interesting to trace the history of a single raindrop! It is not long, geologically speaking, as we have seen, since the first raindrops fell on the newborn leafless Sierra landscapes. How different the lot of these falling now! Happy the showers that fall on so fair a wilderness,— scarce a single drop can fail to find a beautiful spot,—on the tops of the peaks, on the shining glacier pavements, on the great smooth domes, on forests and gardens and brushy moraines, plashing, glinting, pattering, laving. . . . each one of them a high waterfall in itself, descending from the cliffs and hollows of the clouds to the cliffs and hollows of the rocks, out of the sky-thunder into the thunder of the falling rivers. Some . . . patter on grains of gold and heavy way-worn nuggets; some, with blunt plap-plap and low bass drumming, fall on the broad leaves of veratrum, saxifrage, cypripedium. . . . How far they have to go, how many cups to fill, great and small, cells too small to be seen, cups holding half a drop as well as lake basins between the hills, each replenished with equal care, every drop . . . a silvery newborn star with lake and river, garden and grove, valley and mountain, all that the landscape holds reflected in its crystal depths. . . .

Now the storm is over, the sky is clear, the last rolling thunder-wave is spent on the peaks, and where are the raindrops now. . . ? In winged vapor rising some are already hastening back to the sky, some have gone into the plants, creeping through invisible doors into the round rooms of cells, some are locked in crystals of ice, some in rock crystals, some in porous moraines to keep their small springs flowing, some have gone journeying on in the rivers to join the larger raindrop of the ocean. From form to form, beauty to beauty, ever changing, never resting. . . .

Fine calm morning; air tense and clear; not the slightest breeze astir; everything shining, the rocks with wet crystals, the plants with dew, each receiving its portion of irised dewdrops and sunshine like living creatures getting their breakfast, their dew manna coming down from the starry sky like swarms of smaller stars. How wondrous fine are the particles in showers of dew, thousands required for a single drop, growing in the dark as silently as the grass! What pains are taken to keep this wilderness in health,—showers of snow, showers of rain, showers of dew, floods of light, floods of invisible vapor, clouds, winds, all sorts of weather, interaction of plant on plant, animal on animal, etc., beyond thought! How fine Nature's methods! How deeply with beauty is beauty overlaid, the ground covered with crystals, the crystals with mosses and lichens and low-spreading grasses and flowers, these with larger plants leaf over leaf with ever-changing color and form, the broad palms of the firs outspread over these, the azure dome over all like a bell-flower, and star above star.

Yonder stands the South Dome, its crown high above our camp, though its base is four thousand feet below us; a most noble rock, it seems full of thought, clothed with living light, no sense of dead stone about it, all spiritualized, neither heavy looking nor light, steadfast in serene strength like a god.

Our shepherd is a queer character and hard to place in this wilderness. His bed is a hollow made in red dry-rot punky dust beside a log which forms a portion of the south wall of the corral. Here he lies with his wonderful everlasting clothing on, wrapped in a red blanket, breathing not only the dust of the decayed wood but also that of the corral, as if determined to take ammoniacal snuff all night after chewing tobacco all day. Following the sheep he carries a heavy six-shooter swung from his belt on one side and his luncheon on the other. The ancient cloth in which the meat, fresh from the frying-pan, is tied serves as a filter through which the clear fat and gravy juices drip down on his right hip and leg in clustering stalactites. This oleaginous formation is soon broken up, however, and diffused and rubbed evenly into his scanty apparel, by sitting down, rolling over, crossing his legs while resting on logs, etc., making shirt and trousers watertight and shiny. His trousers, in particular, have become so adhesive with the mixed fat and resin that pine needles, thin flakes and fibres of bark, hair, mica scales and minute grains of quartz, hornblende, etc., feathers, seed wings, moth and butterfly wings, legs and antennæ of innumerable insects, or even whole insects such as the small beetles, moths and mosquitoes, with flower petals, pollen dust and indeed bits of all plants, animals, and minerals of the region adhere to them and are safely imbedded, so that though far from being a naturalist he collects fragmentary specimens of everything and becomes richer than he knows. His specimens are kept passably fresh, too, by the purity of the air and the resiny bituminous beds into which they are pressed. Man is a microcosm, at least our shepherd is, or rather his trousers. These precious overalls are never taken off, and nobody knows how old they are, though one may guess by their thickness and concentric structure. Instead of wearing thin they wear thick, and in their stratification have no small geological significance.

Besides herding the sheep, Billy is the butcher, while I have agreed to wash the few iron and tin utensils and make the bread. Then, these small duties done, by the time the sun is fairly above the mountain-tops I am beyond the flock, free to rove and revel in the wilderness all the big immortal days.

Sketching on the North Dome. It commands views of nearly all the valley besides a few of the high mountains. I would fain draw everything in sight—rock, tree, and leaf. But little can I do beyond mere outlines,—marks with meanings like words, readable only to myself,—yet I sharpen my pencils and work on as if others might possibly be benefited. Whether these picture-sheets are to vanish like fallen leaves or go to friends like letters, matters not much; for little can they tell to those who have not themselves seen similar wildness, and like a language have learned it. No pain here, no dull empty hours, no fear of the past, no fear of the future. . . . Drinking this champagne water is pure pleasure, so is breathing the living air, and every movement of limbs is pleasure, while the whole body seems to feel beauty when exposed to it as it feels the campfire or sunshine, entering not by the eyes alone, but equally through all one's flesh like radiant heat, making a passionate ecstatic pleasure-glow not explainable. One's body then seems homogeneous throughout, sound as a crystal.

. . . I gaze and sketch and bask, oftentimes settling down into dumb admiration without definite hope of ever learning much, yet with the longing, unresting effort that lies at the door of hope, humbly prostrate before the vast display of God's power. . . .

. . . The magnitudes of the rocks and trees and streams are so delicately harmonized they are mostly hidden. Sheer precipices three thousand feet high are fringed with tall trees growing close like grass on the brow of a lowland hill, and extending along the feet of these precipices a ribbon of meadow a mile wide and seven or eight long, that seems like a strip a farmer might mow in less than a day. Waterfalls, five hundred to one or two thousand feet high, are so subordinated to the mighty cliffs over which they pour that they seem like wisps of smoke, gentle as floating clouds, though their voices fill the valley and make the rocks tremble.

"... The great Tissiack, or Half-Dome, rising at the upper end of the valley to a height of nearly a mile, is nobly proportioned and life-like, the most impressive of all the rocks, holding the eye in devout admiration, calling it back again and again from falls or meadows, or even the mountains beyond,—marvelous cliffs, marvelous in sheer dizzy depth and sculpture, types of endurance. Thousands of years have they stood in the sky exposed to rain, snow, frost, earthquake and avalanche, yet they still wear the bloom of youth."

...The mountains, too, along the eastern sky, and the domes in front of them, and the succession of smooth rounded waves between, swelling higher, higher, with dark woods in their hollows, serene in massive exuberant bulk and beauty, tend yet more to hide the grandeur of the Yosemite temple and make it appear as a subdued subordinate feature of the vast harmonious landscape. Thus every attempt to appreciate any one feature is beaten down by the overwhelming influence of all the others. . . .

July 21

. . . Saw a common house-fly and a grasshopper and a brown bear. The fly and grasshopper paid me a merry visit on the top of the Dome, and I paid a visit to the bear in the middle of a small garden meadow between the Dome and the camp where he was standing alert among the flowers as if willing to be seen to advantage. . . . I crept to a low ridge of moraine boulders on the edge of a narrow garden meadow, and in this meadow I felt pretty sure the bear must be. I was anxious to get a good look at the sturdy mountaineer without alarming him; so drawing myself up noiselessly back of one of the largest of the trees I peered past its bulging buttresses, exposing only a part of my head, and there stood neighbor Bruin within a stone's throw, his hips covered by tall grass and flowers, and his front feet on the trunk of a fir that had fallen out into the meadow, which raised his head so high that he seemed to be standing erect. He had not yet seen me, but was looking and listening attentively, showing that in some way he was aware of our approach. I watched his gestures and tried to make the most of my opportunity to learn what I could about him, fearing he would catch sight of me and run away. For I had been told that this sort of bear, the cinnamon, always ran from his bad brother man, never showing fight unless wounded or in defense of young. He made a telling picture standing alert in the sunny forest garden. How well he played his part, harmonizing in bulk and color and shaggy hair with the trunks of the trees and lush vegetation, as natural a feature as any other in the landscape. After examining at leisure, noting the sharp muzzle thrust inquiringly forward, the long shaggy hair on his broad chest, the stiff, erect ears nearly buried in hair, and the slow, heavy way he moved his head, I thought I should like to see his gait in running, so I made a sudden rush at him, shouting and swinging my hat to frighten him, expecting to see him make haste to get away. But to my dismay he did not run or show any sign of running. On the contrary, he stood his ground ready to fight and defend himself, lowered his head, thrust it forward, and looked sharply and fiercely at me. Then I suddenly began to fear that upon me would fall the work of running; but I was afraid to run, and therefore, like the bear, held my ground.

We stood staring at each other in solemn silence within a dozen yards or thereabouts, while I fervently hoped that the power of the human eye over wild beasts would prove as great as it is said to be. How long our awfully strenuous interview lasted, I don't know; but at length in the slow fullness of time he pulled his huge paws down off the log, and with magnificent deliberation turned and walked leisurely up the meadow, stopping frequently to look back over his shoulder to see whether I was pursuing him, then moving on again, evidently neither fearing me very much nor trusting me. He was probably about five hundred pounds in weight, a broad, rusty bundle of ungovernable wildness, a happy fellow whose lines have fallen in pleasant places. . . .

. . . I should like to know my hairy brothers better— though after this particular Yosemite bear, my very neighbor, had sauntered out of sight this morning, I reluctantly went back to camp for the Don's rifle to shoot him, if necessary, in defense of the flock. Fortunately I couldn't find him, and after tracking him a mile or two towards Mount Hoffmann I bade him Godspeed and gladly returned to my work on the Yosemite Dome.

The house-fly also seemed at home and buzzed about me as I sat sketching. . . . I wonder what draws house-flies so far up the mountains, heavy gross feeders as they are, sensitive to cold, and fond of domestic ease. How have they been distributed from continent to continent, across seas and deserts and mountain chains, usually so influential in determining boundaries of species both of plants and animals. Beetles and butterflies are sometimes restricted to small areas. Each mountain in a range, and even the different zones of a mountain, may have its own peculiar species. But the house-fly seems to be everywhere. . . .

July 22

A fine specimen of the black-tailed deer went bounding past camp this morning. A buck with wide spread of antlers, showing admirable vigor and grace. Wonderful the beauty, strength, and graceful movements of animals in wildernesses, cared for by Nature only, when our experience with domestic animals would lead us to fear that all the so-called neglected wild beasts would degenerate. Yet the upshot of Nature's method of breeding and teaching seems to lead to excellence of every sort. Deer, like all wild animals, are as clean as plants. The beauties of their gestures and attitudes, alert or in repose, surprise yet more than their bounding exuberant strength. Every movement and posture is graceful, the very poetry of manners and motion. . . .

Have been sketching a silver fir that stands on a granite ridge a few hundred yards to the eastward of camp—a fine tree with a particular snow-storm story to tell. It is about one hundred feet high, growing on bare rock, thrusting its roots into a weathered joint less than an inch wide, and bulging out to form a base to bear its weight. The storm came from the north while it was young and broke it down nearly to the ground, as is shown by the old, dead, weather-beaten top leaning out from the living trunk built up from a new shoot below the break. The annual rings of the trunk that have overgrown the dead sapling tell the year

of the storm. Wonderful that a side branch forming a portion of one of the level collars that encircle the trunk of this species (*Abies magnifica*) should bend upward, grow erect, and take the place of the lost axis to form a new tree.

Many others, pines as well as firs, bear testimony to the crushing severity of this particular storm. Trees, some of them fifty to seventy-five feet high, were bent to the ground and buried like grass, whole groves vanishing as if the forest had been cleared away, leaving not a branch or needle visible until the spring thaw. Then the more elastic undamaged saplings rose again, aided by the wind, some reaching a nearly erect attitude, others remaining more or less bent, while those with broken backs endeavored to specialize a side branch below the break and make a leader of it to form a new axis of development. It is as if a man, whose back was broken or nearly so and who was compelled to go bent, should find a branch backbone sprouting straight up from below the break and should gradually develop new arms and shoulders and head. . . .

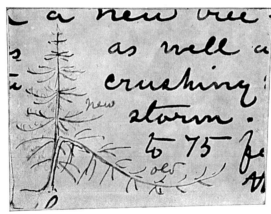

New pine growing from break of snow-crushed tree

"... Every rock in its walls seems to glow with life. Some lean back in majestic repose; others, absolutely sheer or nearly so for thousands of feet, advance beyond their companions in thoughtful attitudes.... Awful in stern, immovable majesty, how softly these rocks are adorned ..."

July 24

Clouds at noon occupying about half the sky gave half an hour of heavy rain to wash one of the cleanest landscapes in the world. How well it is washed! The sea is hardly less dusty than the ice-burnished pavements and ridges, domes and canyons. . . . No wonder the hills and groves were God's first temples, and the more they are cut down and hewn into cathedrals and churches, the farther off and dimmer seems the Lord himself. The same may be said of stone temples. Yonder, to the eastward of our camp grove, stands one of Nature's cathedrals, hewn from the living rock, almost conventional in form, about two thousand feet high, nobly adorned with spires and pinnacles, thrilling under floods of sunshine as if alive like a grove-temple, and well named "Cathedral Peak." Even Shepherd Billy turns at times to this wonderful mountain building, though apparently deaf to all stone sermons. . . . I have been trying to get him to walk to the brink of Yosemite for a view, offering to watch the sheep for a day, while he should enjoy what tourists come from all over the world to see. But though within a mile of the famous valley, he will not go to it even out of mere curiosity. "What," says he, "is Yosemite but a canyon—a lot of rocks—a hole in the ground—a place dangerous about falling into—a d—d good place to keep away from." "But think of the waterfalls, Billy—just think of that big stream we crossed the other day, falling half a mile through the air—think of that, and the sound it makes. You can hear it now like the roar of the sea." Thus I pressed Yosemite upon him like a missionary offering the gospel, but he would have none of it. "I should be afraid to look over so high a wall," he said. "It would make my head swim. There is nothing worth seeing anywhere, only rocks, and I see plenty of them here. Tourists that spend their money to see rocks and falls are fools, that's all. You can't humbug me. I've been in this country too long for that. . . ."

Mount Hoffmann and Lake Tenaya

July 26

Ramble to the summit of Mount Hoffmann, eleven thousand feet high, the highest point in life's journey my feet have yet touched. . . . New plants, new animals, new crystals, and multitudes of new mountains far higher than Hoffmann, towering in glorious array along the axis of the range, serene, majestic, snow-laden, sun-drenched, vast domes and ridges shining below them, forests, lakes, and meadows in the hollows. . . .

Mount Hoffmann is the highest part of a ridge or spur about fourteen miles from the axis of the main range, perhaps a remnant brought into relief and isolated by unequal denudation. The southern slopes shed their waters into Yosemite Valley by Tenaya and Dome Creeks, the northern in part into the Tuolumne River, but mostly into the Merced by Yosemite Creek. The rock is mostly granite, with some small piles and crests rising here and there. . . . Great banks of snow and ice are piled in hollows on the cool precipitous north side forming the highest perennial sources of Yosemite Creek. The southern slopes are much more gradual and accessible. Narrow slot-like gorges extend across the summit at right angles, which look like lanes, formed evidently by the erosion of less resisting beds. They are usually called "devil's slides," though they lie far above the region usually haunted by the devil; for though we read that he once climbed an exceeding high mountain, he cannot be much of a mountaineer, for his tracks are seldom seen above the timberline.

The broad gray summit is barren and desolate-looking in general views, wasted by ages of gnawing storms; but looking at the surface in detail, one finds it covered by thousands and millions of . . . plants with leaves and flowers so small they form no mass of color visible at a distance of a few hundred yards. . . . Here also I found bryanthus, a charming heathwort covered with purple flowers and dark green foliage like heather, and three trees new to me—a hemlock and two pines. The hemlock (*Tsuga Mertensiana*) is the most beautiful conifer I have ever seen; the branches and also the main axis droop in a singularly graceful way, and the dense foliage covers the delicate, sensitive, swaying branchlets all around. It is now in full bloom, and the flowers, together with thousands of last season's cones still clinging to the drooping sprays, display wonderful wealth of color, brown and purple and blue. . . . How wonderful that, with all its delicate feminine grace and beauty of form and dress and behavior, this lovely tree up here, exposed to the wildest blasts, has already endured the storms of centuries of winters! . . .

Tributary of the Tuolumne Canyon, north of the Hoffmann Range

The dwarf or white-bark pine is the species that forms the timberline, where it is so completely dwarfed that one may walk over the top of a bed of it as over snow-pressed chaparral.

How boundless the day seems as we revel in these storm-beaten sky gardens amid so vast a congregation of onlooking mountains! Strange and admirable it is that the more savage and chilly and storm-chafed the mountains, the finer the glow on their faces and the finer the plants they bear. The myriads of flowers tingeing the mountain-top do not seem to have grown out of the dry, rough gravel of disintegration, but rather they appear as visitors, a cloud of witnesses to Nature's love in what we in our timid ignorance and unbelief call howling desert. The surface of the ground, so dull and forbidding at first sight, besides being rich in plants, shines and sparkles with crystals: mica, hornblende, feldspar, quartz, tourmaline. . . .

From garden to garden, ridge to ridge, I drifted enchanted, now on my knees gazing into the face of a daisy, now climbing again and again among the purple and azure flowers of the hemlocks, now down into the treasuries of the snow, or gazing afar over domes and peaks, lakes and woods, and the billowy glaciated fields of the upper Tuolumne, and trying to sketch them. In the midst of such beauty, pierced with its rays, one's body is all one tingling palate. Who wouldn't be a mountaineer! Up here all the world's prizes seem nothing.

The largest of the many glacier lakes in sight, and the one with the finest shore scenery, is Tenaya, about a mile long, with an imposing mountain dipping its feet into it on the south side, Cathedral Peak a few miles above its head, many smooth swelling rock-waves and domes on the north, and in the distance southward a multitude of snowy peaks, the fountain-heads of rivers. Lake Hoffmann lies shimmering beneath my feet, mountain pines around its shining rim. To the northward the picturesque basin of Yosemite Creek glitters with lakelets and pools; but the eye is soon drawn away from these bright mirror wells, however attractive, to revel in the glorious congregation of peaks on the axis of the range in their robes of snow and light. . . .

July 27

. . . Am holding an easterly course, the deep canyon of Tenaya Creek on the right hand, Mount Hoffmann on

Tenaya Lake and Cathedral Peak

the left, and the lake straight ahead about ten miles distant, the summit of Mount Hoffmann about three thousand feet above me, Tenaya Creek four thousand feet below and separated from the shallow, irregular valley, along which most of the way lies, by smooth domes and wave-ridges. Many mossy emerald bogs, meadows, and gardens in rocky hollows to wade and saunter through . . .

. . . No Sierra landscape that I have seen holds anything truly dead or dull, or any trace of what in manufactories is

called rubbish or waste. . . . When we try to pick out anything by itself, we find it hitched to everything else in the universe. One fancies a heart like our own must be beating in every crystal and cell. . . .

I found three kinds of meadows: (1) Those contained in basins not yet filled with earth enough to make a dry surface. . . . (2) Those contained in the same sort of basins, once lakes like the first, but so situated in relation

Glacier meadow, headwaters of the Tuolumne

to the streams that flow through them and beds of transportable sand, gravel, etc., that they are now high and dry and well drained. This dry condition and corresponding difference in their vegetation may be caused by no superiority of position, or power of transporting filling material in the streams that belong to them, but simply by the basin being shallow and therefore sooner filled. . . . (3) Meadows hanging on ridge and mountain slopes, not in basins at all, but made and held in place by masses of boulders and fallen trees, which, forming dams one above another in close succession on small, outspread, channel-less streams, have collected soil enough for the growth of grasses, carices, and many flowering plants, and being kept well watered, without being subject to currents sufficiently strong to carry them away, a hanging or sloping meadow is the result. Their surfaces are seldom so smooth as the others, being roughened more or less by the projecting tops of the dam rocks or logs; but at a little distance this roughness is not noticed, and the effect is very striking —bright green, fluent, down-sweeping flowery ribbons on gray slopes. The broad shallow streams these meadows belong to are mostly derived from banks of snow. . . . These meadows are now in their prime. How wonderful must be the temper of the elastic leaves of grasses and sedges to make curves so perfect and fine. Tempered a little harder, they would stand erect, stiff and bristly, like strips of metal; a little softer, and every leaf would lie flat.

The principal tree for the first mile or two from camp is the magnificent silver fir, which reaches perfection here both in size and form of individual trees, and in the mode of grouping in groves with open spaces between. So trim and tasteful are these silvery, spiry groves one would fancy they must have been placed in position by some master landscape gardener, their regularity seeming almost conventional. . . . Higher, the firs gradually become smaller and less perfect, many showing double summits,

Mount Clark   South Dome   Mount Starr King
Abies Magnifica

indicating storm stress. Still, where good moraine soil is found, even on the rim of the lake-basin, specimens one hundred and fifty feet in height and five feet in diameter occur nearly nine thousand feet above the sea. The saplings, I find, are mostly bent with the crushing weight of the winter snow, which at this elevation must be at least eight or ten feet deep, judging by marks on the trees; and this depth of compacted snow is heavy enough to bend and bury young trees twenty or thirty feet in height and hold them down for four or five months. Some are broken; the others spring up when the snow melts and at length attain a size that enables them to withstand the snow pressure. Yet even in trees five feet thick the traces of this early discipline are still plainly to be seen in their curved in-steps, and frequently in old dried saplings protruding from the trunk, partially overgrown by the new axis developed from a branch below the break. Yet through all this stress the forest is maintained in marvelous beauty.

Beyond the silver firs I find the two-leaved pine (*Pinus contorta,* var. *Murrayana*) forms the bulk of the forest up

to an elevation of ten thousand feet or more—the highest timberbelt of the Sierra. I saw a specimen nearly five feet in diameter growing on deep, well-watered soil at an elevation of about nine thousand feet. . . .

A still hardier mountaineer is the Sierra juniper (*Juniperus occidentalis*), growing mostly on domes and ridges and glacier pavements. A thickset, sturdy, picturesque highlander, seemingly content to live for more than a score of centuries on sunshine and snow. . . . Some are nearly as broad as high. I saw one on the shore of the lake nearly ten feet in diameter, and many six to eight feet. . . . it never seems to die a natural death, or even to fall after it has been killed. If protected from accidents, it would perhaps be immortal. I saw some that had withstood an avalanche from snowy Mount Hoffmann cheerily putting out new branches. . . . Some were simply standing on the pavement where no fissure more than half an inch wide offered a hold for its roots. The common height for these rock-dwellers is from ten to twenty feet; most of the old ones have broken tops, and are mere stumps, with a few tufted branches, forming picturesque brown pillars on bare pavements, with plenty of elbow-room and a clear view in every direction. On good moraine soil it reaches a height of from forty to sixty feet, with dense gray foliage. The rings of the trunk are very thin, eighty to an inch of diameter in some specimens I examined. Those ten feet in diameter must be very old—thousands of years. . . .

The lake was named for one of the chiefs of the Yosemite tribe. Old Tenaya is said to have been a good Indian to his tribe. When a company of soldiers followed his band into Yosemite to punish them for cattle-stealing and other crimes, they fled to this lake by a trail that leads out of the upper end of the valley, early in the spring, while the snow was still deep; but being pursued, they lost heart and surrendered. A fine monument the old man has in this bright lake, and likely to last a long time, though lakes die as well as Indians, being gradually filled with detritus carried in by the feeding streams, and to some extent also by snow avalanches and rain and wind. A considerable portion of the Tenaya basin is already changed into a forested flat and meadow at the upper end, where the main tributary enters from Cathedral Peak. Two other tributaries come from the Hoffmann Range. The outlet flows westward through Tenaya Canyon to join the Merced River in Yosemite. Scarce a handful of loose soil is to be seen on the north shore. All is bare, shining granite, suggesting the Indian name of the lake, Pywiack, meaning shining rock. The basin seems to have been slowly excavated by the ancient glaciers. . . . On the south side an imposing mountain rises from the water's edge to a height of three thousand feet or more, feathered with hemlock and pine; and huge shining domes on the east, over the tops of which the grinding, wasting, molding glacier must have swept as the wind does to-day.

July 28

. . . Have been studying the *magnifica* fir—measured one near two hundred and forty feet high, the tallest I have yet seen. This species is the most symmetrical of all conifers, but though gigantic in size it seldom lives more than four or five hundred years. Most of the trees die from the attacks of a fungus at the age of two or three centuries. This dry-rot fungus perhaps enters the trunk by way of the stumps of limbs broken off by the snow that loads the broad palmate branches. The younger specimens are marvels of symmetry, straight and erect as a plumb-line, their branches in regular level whorls of five mostly, each branch as exact in its divisions as a fern frond. . . .

. . . The cones are grand affairs, superb in form, size, and color, cylindrical, stand erect on the upper branches like casks, and are from five to eight inches in length by three or four in diameter, greenish gray, and covered with fine down which has a silvery luster in the sunshine, and their brilliance is augmented by beads of transparent balsam which seems to have been poured over each cone, bringing to mind the old ceremonies of anointing with oil. If possible, the inside of the cone is more beautiful than the outside; the scales, bracts, and seed wings are tinted with the loveliest rosy purple with a bright lustrous iridescence; the seeds, three-fourths of an inch long, are dark brown. When the cones are ripe the scales and bracts fall off, setting the seeds free to fly to their predestined places, while the dead spike-like axes are left on the branches for many years to mark the positions of the vanished cones, excepting those cut off when green by the Douglas squirrel. How he gets his teeth under the broad bases of the sessile cones, I don't know. . . .

July 30

. . . Ants, flies, and mosquitoes seem to enjoy this fine climate. A few house-flies have discovered our camp. The Sierra mosquitoes are courageous and of good size, some of them measuring nearly an inch from tip of sting to tip of folded wings. Though less abundant than in most wildernesses, they occasionally make quite a hum and stir, and pay but little attention to time or place. They sting anywhere, any time of day, wherever they can find anything worth while, until they are themselves stung by frost. The large, jet-black ants are only ticklish and troublesome when one is lying down under the trees.

Noticed a borer drilling a silver fir. Ovipositor about an inch and a half in length, polished and straight like a needle. When not in use, it is folded back in a sheath, which extends straight behind like the legs of a crane in flying. This drilling, I suppose, is to save nest building, and the after care of feeding the young. Who would guess that in the brain of a fly so much knowledge could find lodgment? How do they know that their eggs will hatch in such holes, or, after they hatch, that the soft, helpless grubs will find the right sort of nourishment in silver fir sap? This domestic arrangement calls to mind the curious family of gallflies. Each species seems to know what kind of plant will respond to the irritation or stimulus of the puncture it makes and the eggs it lays, in forming a growth that not only answers for a nest and home but also provides food for the young. Probably these gallflies make mistakes at times, like anybody else; but when they do, there is simply a failure of that particular brood, while enough to perpetuate the species do find the proper plants and nourishment. Many mistakes of this kind might be made without being discovered by us. Once a pair of wrens made the mistake of building a nest in the sleeve of a workman's coat, which was called for at sundown, much to the consternation and discomfiture of the birds. Still the marvel remains that any of the children of such small people as gnats and mosquitoes should escape their own and their parents' mistakes, as well as the vicissitudes of the weather and hosts of enemies, and come forth in full vigor and perfection to enjoy the sunny world. When we think of the small creatures that are visible, we are led to think of many that are smaller still and lead us on and on into infinite mystery.

July 31

Another glorious day, the air as delicious to the lungs as nectar to the tongue; indeed the body seems one palate, and tingles equally throughout. . . .

The cheery little chipmunk so common about Brown's Flat is common here also, and perhaps other species. In their light, airy habits they recall the familiar species of the Eastern States, which we admired in the oak openings of Wisconsin as they skimmed along the zigzag rail fences. These Sierra chipmunks are more arboreal and squirrel-like. I first noticed them on the lower edge of the coniferous belt, where the Sabine and yellow pines meet—exceedingly interesting little fellows, full of odd, funny ways, and without being true squirrels, have most of their accomplishments without their aggressive quarrelsomeness. I never weary watching them as they frisk about in the bushes gathering seeds and berries, like song sparrows poising daintily on slender twigs, and making even less stir than most birds of the same size. . . . They seem dearly to love teasing a dog, coming frequently almost within reach, then frisking away with lively chipping, like sparrows, beating time to their music with their tails, which at each chip describe half circles from side to side. Not even the Douglas squirrel is surer-footed or more fearless. I have seen them running about on sheer precipices of the Yosemite walls seemingly holding on with as little effort as flies, and as unconscious of danger, where, if the slightest slip were made, they would have fallen two or three thousand feet. How fine it would be could we mountaineers climb these tremendous cliffs with the same sure grip! The venture I made the other day for a view of the Yosemite Fall, and which tried my nerves so sorely, this little Tamias would have made for an ear of grass.

The woodchuck (*Arctomys monax*) of the bleak mountain-tops is a very different sort of mountaineer—the most bovine of rodents, a heavy eater, fat, aldermanic in bulk and fairly bloated, in his high pastures, like a cow in a clover field. One woodchuck would outweigh a hundred chipmunks, and yet he is by no means a dull animal. In the midst of what we regard as storm-beaten desolation he pipes and whistles right cheerily, and enjoys long life in his skyland homes. His burrow is made in disintegrated rocks or beneath large boulders. Coming out of his den in the cold hoarfrost mornings, he takes a sun-bath on some favorite flat-topped rock, then goes to breakfast in garden hollows, eats grass and flowers until comfortably swollen, then goes a-visiting to fight and play. How long a woodchuck lives in this bracing air I don't know, but some of them are rusty and gray like lichen-covered boulders.

August 1

. . . The mountain quail (*Oreortyx ricta*) I often meet in my walks—a small brown partridge with a very long, slender, ornamental crest worn jauntily like a feather in a boy's cap, giving it a very marked appearance. This species is considerably larger than the valley quail, so common on the hot foothills. They seldom alight in trees, but love to wander in flocks of from five to six to twenty through the ceanothus and manzanita thickets and over open, dry meadows and rocks of the ridges where the forest is less dense or wanting, uttering a low clucking sound to enable them to keep together. When disturbed they rise with a strong birr of wing-beats, and scatter as if exploded to a distance of a quarter of a mile or so. . . . I wonder how they live through the long winters, when the ground is snow-covered ten feet deep. They must go down towards the lower edge of the forest, like the deer, though I have not heard of them there.

The blue, or dusky, grouse is also common here. They like the deepest and closest fir woods, and when disturbed, burst from the branches of the trees with a strong, loud whir of wing-beats, and vanish in a wavering, silent slide, without moving a feather—a stout, beautiful bird about the size of the prairie chicken of the old west, spending most of the time in the trees, excepting the breeding season, when it keeps to the ground. The young are now able to fly. When scattered by man or dog, they keep still until the danger is supposed to be passed, then the mother calls them together. The chicks can hear the call a distance of several hundred yards, though it is not loud. Should the young be unable to fly, the mother feigns desperate lameness or death to draw one away, throwing herself at one's feet within two or three yards, rolling over on her back, kicking and gasping, so as to deceive man or beast. They are said to stay all the year in the woods hereabouts, taking shelter in dense tufted branches of fir and yellow pine during snowstorms, and feeding on the young buds of these trees. Their legs are feathered down to their toes, and I have never heard of their suffering in any sort of weather. Able to live on pine and fir buds, they are forever independent in the matter of food, which troubles so many of us and controls our movements. Gladly, if I could, I would live forever on pine buds, however full of turpentine and pitch, for the sake of this grand independence. Just to think of our sufferings last month merely for grist-mill flour. Man seems to have more difficulty in gaining food than any other of the Lord's creatures. For many in towns it is a consuming, lifelong struggle; for others, the danger of coming to want is so great, the deadly habit of endless hoarding for the future is formed, which smothers all real life, and is continued long after every reasonable need has been over-supplied.

On Mount Hoffmann I saw a curious dove-colored bird that seemed half woodpecker, half magpie, or crow. It screams something like a crow, but flies like a woodpecker, and has a long, straight bill, with which I saw it opening the cones of the mountain and white-barked pines. It seems to keep to the heights, though no doubt it comes down for shelter during winter, if not for food. So far as food is concerned, these bird-mountaineers, I guess, can glean nuts enough, even in winter, from the different kinds of conifers; for always there are a few that have been unable to fly out of the cones and remain for hungry winter gleaners.

The Middle Ranges

"Noble mountains rise close about me,
    and far southward are the highest of the range
    with glaciers on their sides.
A stream sings lonely."

"... The sculpture of the landscape is as striking in its main lines as in its lavish richness of detail.... The whole landscape showed design, like man's noblest sculptures. How wonderful the power of its beauty!"

"... Through this flowery lawn flows a stream silently gliding, swirling, slipping as if careful not to make the slightest noise."

". . . Every raincloud, however fleeting, leaves its mark,
not only on trees and flowers whose pulses are quickened,
and on the replenished streams and lakes, but also on the
rocks are its marks engraved whether we can see them
or not . . ."

"... New plants, new animals, new crystals, and multitudes of new mountains far higher, ... towering in glorious array along the axis of the range, serene, majestic, snow-laden, sun-drenched, vast domes and ridges shining below them, forests, lakes, and meadows in the hollows."

". . . out of this bower the creek, grown strong with
many indashing tributaries, leaps forth into the light,
and descends in a fluted curve thick-sown with crisp flashing spray."

"... rocky strength and permanence combined with beauty of plants frail and fine and evanescent; water descending in thunder, and the same water gliding through meadows and groves in gentlest beauty."

A Strange Experience

Clouds and showers, about the same as yesterday. Sketching all day on the North Dome until four or five o'clock in the afternoon, when, as I was busily employed thinking only of the glorious Yosemite landscape, trying to draw every tree and every line and feature of the rocks, I was suddenly, and without warning, possessed with the notion that my friend, Professor J. D. Butler, of the State University of Wisconsin, was below me in the valley, and I jumped up full of the idea of meeting him, with almost as much startling excitement as if he had suddenly touched me to make me look up. Leaving my work without the slightest deliberation, I ran down the western slope of the Dome and along the brink of the valley wall, looking for a way to the bottom, until I came to a side canyon, which judging by its apparently continuous growth of trees and bushes, I thought might afford a practical way into the valley, and immediately began to make the descent, late as it was, as if drawn irresistibly. But after a little, common sense stopped me and explained that it would be long after dark ere I could possibly reach the hotel, that the visitors would be asleep, that nobody would know me, that I had no money in my pockets, and moreover was without a coat. I therefore compelled myself to stop, and finally succeeded in reasoning myself out of the notion of seeking my friend in the dark, whose presence I only felt in a strange, telepathic way. I succeeded in dragging myself back through the woods to camp, never for a moment wavering, however, in my determination to go down to him next morning. This I think is the most unexplainable notion that ever struck me. Had some one whispered in my ear while I sat on the Dome, where I had spent so many days, that Professor Butler was in the valley, I could not have been more surprised and startled. When I was leaving the university, he said, "Now, John, I want to hold you in sight and watch your career. Promise to write me at least once a year." I received a letter from him in July, at our first camp in the Hollow, written in May, in which he said that he might possibly visit California some time this summer, and therefore hoped to meet me. But inasmuch as he named no meeting-place, and gave no directions as to the course he would probably follow, and as I should be in the wilderness all summer, I had not the slightest hope of seeing him, and all thought of the matter had vanished from my mind until this afternoon, when he seemed to be wafted bodily almost against my face. Well, to-morrow I shall see; for, reasonable or unreasonable, I feel I must go.

August 3

Had a wonderful day. Found Professor Butler as the compass-needle finds the pole. So last evening's telepathy, transcendental revelation, or whatever else it may be called, was true; for, strange to say, he had just entered the valley by way of the Coulterville Trail and was coming up the valley past El Capitan when his presence struck me. Had he then looked toward the North Dome with a good glass when it first came in sight, he might have seen me jump up from my work and run toward him. This seems the one well-defined marvel of my life of the kind called supernatural; for, absorbed in glad Nature, spirit-rappings, second sight, ghost stories, etc., have never interested me since boyhood, seeming comparatively useless and infinitely less wonderful than Nature's open, harmonious, songful, sunny, everyday beauty.

This morning, when I thought of having to appear among tourists at a hotel, I was troubled because I had no suitable clothes, and at best am desperately bashful and shy. I was determined to go, however, to see my old friend after two years among strangers; got on a clean pair of overalls, a cashmere shirt, and a sort of jacket,—the best my camp wardrobe afforded,—tied my notebook on my belt, and strode away on my strange journey, followed by Carlo. I made my way though the gap discovered last evening, which proved to be Indian Canyon. There was no trail in it, and the rocks and brush were so rough that Carlo frequently called me back to help him down precipitous places. Emerging from the canyon shadows, I found a man making hay on one of the meadows, and asked him whether Professor Butler was in the valley. "I don't know," he replied; "but you can easily find out at the hotel. There are but few visitors in the valley just now. A small party came in yesterday afternoon, and I heard some one called Professor Butler, or Butterfield, or some name like that."

In front of the gloomy hotel I found a tourist party adjusting their fishing tackle. They all stared at me in silent wonderment, as if I had been seen dropping down through the trees from the clouds, mostly, I suppose, on account of my strange garb. Inquiring for the office, I was told it was locked, and that the landlord was away, but I might find the landlady, Mrs. Hutchings, in the parlor. I entered in a sad state of embarrassment, and after I had waited in the big, empty room and knocked at several doors the landlady at length appeared, and in reply to my question said she rather thought Professor Butler *was* in the valley, but to make sure, she would bring the register from the office. Among the names of the last arrivals I soon discovered the Professor's familiar handwriting, at the sight of which bashfulness vanished; and having learned that his party had gone up the valley,—probably to the Vernal and Nevada Falls,—I pushed on in glad pursuit, my heart now sure of its prey. In less than an hour I reached the head of the Nevada Canyon at the Vernal Fall, and just outside of the spray discovered a distinguished-looking gentleman, who, like everybody else I have seen to-day, regarded me curiously as I approached. When I made bold to inquire if he knew where Professor Butler was, he seemed yet more curious to know what could possibly have happened that required a messenger for the Professor, and instead of answering my question he asked with military sharpness, "Who wants him?" "I want him," I replied with equal sharpness. "Why? Do *you* know him?" "Yes," I said. "Do *you* know him?" Astonished that any one in the mountains could possibly know Professor Butler and find him as soon as he had reached the valley, he came down to meet the strange mountaineer on equal terms, and courteously replied, "Yes, I know Professor Butler very well. I am General Alvord, and we were fellow students in Rutland, Vermont, long ago, when we were both young." "But where is he now?" I persisted, cutting short his story. "He has gone beyond the falls with a companion, to try to climb that big rock, the top of which you see from here." His guide now volunteered the information that it was the Liberty Cap Professor Butler and his companion had gone to climb, and that if I waited at the head of the fall I should be sure to find them on their way down. I therefore climbed the ladders alongside the Vernal Fall, and was pushing foward, determined to go to the top of Liberty Cap rock in my hurry, rather than wait, if I should

not meet my friend sooner. So heart-hungry at times may one be to see a friend in the flesh, however happily full and care-free one's life may be. I had gone but a short distance, however, above the brow of the Vernal Fall when I caught sight of him in the brush and rocks, half erect, groping his way, his sleeves rolled up, vest open, hat in his hand, evidently very hot and tired. When he saw me coming he sat down on a boulder to wipe the perspiration from his brow and neck, and taking me for one of the valley guides, he inquired the way to the fall ladders. I pointed out the path marked with little piles of stones, on seeing which he called his companion, saying that the way was found; but he did not yet recognize me. Then I stood directly in front of him, looked him in the face, and held out my hand. He thought I was offering to assist him in rising. "Never mind," he said. Then I said, "Professor Butler, don't you know me?" "I think not," he replied; but catching my eye, sudden recognition followed, and astonishment that I should have found him just when he was lost in the brush and did not know that I was within hundreds of miles of him. "John Muir, John Muir, where have you come from?" Then I told him the story of my feeling his presence when he entered the valley last evening, when he was four or five miles distant, as I sat sketching on the North Dome. This, of course, only made him wonder the more. Below the foot of the Vernal Fall the guide was waiting with his saddle-horse, and I walked along the trail, chatting all the way back to the hotel, talking of school days, friends in Madison, of the students, how each had prospered, etc., ever and anon gazing at the stupendous rocks about us, now growing indistinct in the gloaming, and again quoting from the poets—a rare ramble.

It was late ere we reached the hotel, and General Alvord was waiting the Professor's arrival for dinner. When I was introduced he seemed yet more astonished than the Professor at my descent from cloudland and going straight to my friend without knowing in any ordinary way that he was even in California. They had come on direct from the East, had not yet visited any of their friends in the state, and considered themselves undiscoverable. As we sat at dinner, the General leaned back in his chair, and looking down the table, thus introduced me to the dozen guests or so, including the staring fisherman mentioned above: "This man, you know, came down out of these huge, trackless mountains, you know, to find his friend Professor Butler here, the very day he arrived; and how did he know he was here? He just felt him, he says. This is the queerest case of Scotch farsightedness I ever heard of," etc., etc. While my friend quoted Shakespeare: "More things in heaven and earth, Horatio, than are dreamt of in your philosophy," "As the sun, ere he has risen, sometimes paints his image in the firmament, e'en so the shadows of events precede the events, and in to-day already walks to-morrow."

Had a long conversation, after dinner, over Madison days. The Professor wants me to promise to go with him, sometime, on a camping trip in the Hawaiian Islands, while I tried to get him to go back with me to camp in the high Sierra. But he says, "Not now." He must not leave the General; and I was surprised to learn they are to leave the valley to-morrow or next day. I'm glad I'm not great enough to be missed in the busy world.

August 4

It seemed strange to sleep in a paltry hotel chamber after the spacious magnificence and luxury of the starry sky and silver fir grove. Bade farewell to my friend and the General. The old soldier was very kind, and an interesting talker. He told me long stories of the Florida Seminole war, in which he took part, and invited me to visit him in Omaha. Calling Carlo, I scrambled home through the Indian Canyon gate, rejoicing, pitying the poor Professor and General, bound by clocks, almanacs, orders, duties, etc., and compelled to dwell with lowland care and dust and din, where Nature is covered and her voice smothered, while the poor, insignificant wanderer enjoys the freedom and glory of God's wilderness.

Apart from the human interest of my visit to-day, I greatly enjoyed Yosemite, which I had visited only once before, having spent eight days last spring in rambling amid its rocks and waters. Wherever we go in the mountains, or indeed in any of God's wild fields, we find more than we seek. Descending four thousand feet in a few hours, we enter a new world—climate, plants, sounds, inhabitants, and scenery all new or changed. Near camp the goldcup oak forms sheets of chaparral, on top of which we may make our beds. Going down the Indian Canyon we observe this little bush changing by regular gradations to a large bush, to a small tree, and then larger, until on the rocky taluses near the bottom of the valley we find it developed into a broad, wide-spreading, gnarled, picturesque tree from four to eight feet in diameter, and forty or fifty feet high. Innumerable are the forms of water displayed. Every gliding reach, cascade, and fall has characters of its own. Had a good view of the Vernal and Nevada, two of the main falls of the valley, less than a mile apart, and offering striking differences in voice, form, color, etc. The Vernal, four hundred feet high and about seventy-five or eighty feet wide, drops smoothly over a round-lipped precipice and forms a superb apron of embroidery, green and white, slightly folded and fluted, maintaining this form nearly to the bottom, where it is suddenly veiled in quick-flying billows of spray and mist, in which the afternoon sunbeams play with ravishing beauty of rainbow colors. The Nevada is white from its appearance as it leaps out into the freedom of the air. At the head it presents a twisted appearance, by an overfolding of the current from striking on the side of its channel just before the first free outbounding leap is made. About two-thirds of the way down, the hurrying throng of comet-shaped masses glance on an inclined part of the face of the precipice and are beaten into yet whiter foam, greatly expanded, and sent bounding outward, making an indescribably glorious show, especially when the afternoon sunshine is pouring into it. In this fall—one of the most wonderful in the world—the water does not seem to be under the dominion of ordinary laws, but rather as if it were a living creature, full of the strength of the mountains and their huge, wild joy.

From beneath heavy throbbing blasts of spray the broken river is seen emerging in ragged boulder-chafed strips. These are speedily gathered into a roaring torrent, showing that the young river is still gloriously alive. On it goes, shouting, roaring, exulting in its strength, passes through a gorge with sublime display of energy, then suddenly expands on a gently inclined pavement, down which it rushes in thin sheets and folds of lace-work into a quiet pool,—"Emerald Pool," as it is called,—a stopping-place, a period separating two grand sentences. Resting here long enough to part with its foam-bells and gray mixtures of air, it glides quietly to the verge of the Vernal precipice in a broad sheet and makes its new display in the Vernal Fall; then more rapids and rock tossings down the canyon, shaded by live oak, Douglas spruce, fir, maple, and dogwood. It receives the Illilouette tributary, and makes a long sweep out into the level, sun-filled valley to join the other streams which, like itself, have danced and sung their way down from snowy heights to form the main Merced—the river of Mercy. But of this there is no end, and life, when one thinks of it, is so short. Never mind, one day in the midst of these divine glories is well worth living and toiling and striving for. . . .

It seems strange that visitors to Yosemite should be so little influenced by its novel grandeur, as if their eyes were bandaged and their ears stopped. Most of those I saw yesterday were looking down as if wholly unconscious of anything going on about them, while the sublime rocks were trembling with the tones of the mighty chanting congregation of waters gathered from all the mountains round about, making music that might draw angels out of heaven. Yet respectable-looking, even wise-looking people were fixing bits of worms on bent pieces of wire to catch trout. Sport they called it. . . .

Now I'm back at the camp-fire, and cannot help thinking about my recognition of my friend's presence in the valley while he was four or five miles away, and while I had no means of knowing that he was not thousands of miles away. It seems supernatural, but only because it is not understood. Anyhow, it seems silly to make so much of it, while the natural and common is more truly marvelous and mysterious than the so-called supernatural. Indeed most of the miracles we hear of are infinitely less wonderful than the commonest of natural phenomena, when fairly seen. Perhaps the invisible rays that struck me while I sat at work on the Dome are something like those which attract and repel people at first sight, concerning which so much nonsense has been written. The worst apparent effect of these mysterious odd things is blindness to all that is divinely common. Hawthorne, I fancy, could weave one of his weird romances out of this little telepathic episode, the one strange marvel of my life, probably replacing my good old Professor by an attractive woman.

August 5

We were awakened this morning before daybreak by the furious barking of Carlo and Jack and the sound of stampeding sheep. Billy fled from his punk bed to the fire, and refused to stir into the darkness to try to gather the scattered flock, or ascertain the nature of the disturbance. It was a bear attack, as we afterward learned, and I suppose little was gained by attempting to do anything before daylight. Nevertheless, being anxious to know what was up, Carlo and I groped our way through the woods, guided by the rustling sound made by fragments of the flock, not fearing the bear, for I knew that the runaways would go from their enemy as far as possible and Carlo's nose was also to be depended upon. About half a mile east of the corral we overtook twenty or thirty of the flock and succeeded in driving them back; then turning to the westward, we traced another band of fugitives and got them back to the flock. After daybreak I discovered the remains of a sheep carcass, still warm, showing that Bruin must have been enjoying his early mutton breakfast while I was seeking the runaways. He had eaten about half of it. Six dead sheep lay in the corral, evidently smothered by the crowding and piling up of the flock against the side of the corral wall when the bear entered. Making a wide circuit of the camp, Carlo and I discovered a third band of fugitives and drove them back to camp. We also discovered another dead sheep half eaten, showing there had been two of the shaggy freebooters at this early breakfast. They were easily traced. They had each caught a sheep, jumped over the corral fence with them, carrying them as a cat carries a mouse, laid them at the foot of fir trees a hundred yards or so back from the corral, and eaten their fill. After breakfast I set out to seek more of the lost, and found seventy-five at a considerable distance from camp. In the afternoon I succeeded, with Carlo's help, in getting them back to the flock. I don't know whether all are together again or not. I shall make a big fire this evening and keep watch.

When I asked Billy why he made his bed against the corral in rotten wood, when so many better places offered, he replied that he "wished to be as near the sheep as possible in case bears should attack them." Now that the bears have come, he has moved his bed to the far side of the camp, and seems afraid that he may be mistaken for a sheep.

This has been mostly a sheep day, and of course studies have been interrupted. Nevertheless, the walk through the gloom of the woods before the dawn was worth while, and I have learned something about these noble bears. Their tracks are very telling, and so are their breakfasts. . . .

August 6

Enjoyed the grand illumination of the camp grove, last night, from the fire we made to frighten the bears—compensation for loss of sleep and sheep. The noble pillars of verdure, vividly aglow, seemed to shoot into the sky like the flames and lighted them. Nevertheless, one of the bears paid us another visit, as if more attracted than repelled by the fire, climbed into the corral, killed a sheep and made off with it without being seen, while still another was lost by trampling and suffocation against the side of the corral. Now that our mutton has been tasted, I suppose it will be difficult to put a stop to the ravages of these freebooters.

The Don arrived to-day from the lowlands with provisions and a letter. On learning the losses he had sustained, he determined to move the flock at once to the Upper Tuolumne region, saying that the bears would be sure to visit the camp every night as long as we stayed, and that no fire or noise we might make would avail to frighten them. No clouds save a few thin, lustrous touches on the eastern horizon. Thunder heard in the distance.

The Mono Trail

Early this morning bade good-bye to the bears and blessed silver fir camp, and moved slowly eastward along the Mono Trail. At sundown camped for the night on one of the many small flowery meadows so greatly enjoyed on my excursion to Lake Tenaya. The dusty, noisy flock seems outrageously foreign and out of place in these nature gardens, more so than bears among sheep. The harm they do goes to the heart, but glorious hope lifts above all the dust and din and bids me look forward to a good time coming, when money enough will be earned to enable me to go walking where I like in pure wildness, with what I can carry on my back, and when the bread-sack is empty, run down to the nearest point on the bread-line for more. Nor will these run-downs be blanks, for, whether up or down, every step and jump on these blessed mountains is full of fine lessons.

August 8

Camp at the west end of Lake Tenaya. Arriving early, I took a walk on the glacier-polished pavements along the north shore, and climbed the magnificent mountain rock at the east end of the lake, now shining in the late afternoon light. Almost every yard of its surface shows the scoring and polishing action of a great glacier that enveloped it and swept heavily over its summit, though it is about two thousand feet high above the lake and ten thousand above sea-level. This majestic, ancient ice-flood came from the eastward, as the scoring and crushing of the surface shows. Even below the waters of the lake the rock in some places is still grooved and polished; the lapping of the waves and their disintegrating action have not as yet obliterated even the superficial marks of glaciation. In climbing the steepest polished places I had to take off shoes and stockings. A fine region this for study of glacial action in mountain-making. . . .

Made sketch of the lake, and sauntered back to camp, my iron-shod shoes clanking on the pavements disturbing the chipmunks and birds. After dark went out to the shore,—not a breath of air astir, the lake a perfect mirror reflecting the sky and mountains with their stars and trees and wonderful sculpture, all their grandeur refined and doubled,—a marvelously impressive picture, that seemed to belong more to heaven than earth.

August 9

I went ahead of the flock, and crossed over the divide between the Merced and Tuolumne Basins. The gap between the east end of the Hoffmann spur and the mass of mountain rocks about Cathedral Peak, though roughened by ridges and waving folds, seems to be one of the channels of a broad ancient glacier that came from the mountains on the summit of the range. In crossing this divide the ice-river made an ascent of about five hundred feet from the Tuolumne meadows. This entire region must have been overswept by ice.

From the top of the divide, and also from the big Tuolumne Meadows, the wonderful mountain called Cathedral Peak is in sight. From every point of view it shows marked individuality. It is a majestic temple of one stone, hewn from the living rock, and adorned with spires and pinnacles in regular cathedral style. The dwarf pines on the roof look like mosses. I hope some time to climb to it to say my prayers and hear the stone sermons.

The big Tuolumne Meadows are flowery lawns, lying along the south fork of the Tuolumne River at a height of about eighty-five hundred to nine thousand feet above the sea, partially separated by forests and bars of glaciated granite. Here the mountains seem to have been cleared away or set back, so that wide-open views may be had in every direction. The upper end of the series lies at the base of Mount Lyell, the lower below the east end of the Hoffmann Range, so the length must be about ten or twelve miles. They vary in width from a quarter of a mile to perhaps three quarters, and a good many branch meadows put out along the banks of the tributary streams. This is the most spacious and delightful high pleasure-ground I have yet seen. The air is keen and bracing, yet warm during the day; and though lying high in the sky, the surrounding mountains are so much higher, one feels protected as if in a grand hall. Mounts Dana and Gibbs, massive red mountains, perhaps thirteen thousand feet high or more, bound the view on the east, the Cathedral and Unicorn Peaks, with many nameless peaks, on the south, the Hoffmann Range on the west, and a number of peaks unnamed, as far as I know, on the north. One of these last is much like the Cathedral. The grass of the meadows is mostly fine and silky, with exceedingly slender leaves, making a close sod, above which the panicles of minute purple flowers seem to float in airy, misty lightness. . . .

On the return trip I met the flock about three miles east of Lake Tenaya. Here we camped for the night near a small lake lying on top of the divide in a clump of the two-leaved pine. We are now about nine thousand feet above the sea. Small lakes abound in all sorts of situations, —on ridges, along mountain sides, and in piles of moraine boulders, most of them mere pools. Only in those canyons of the larger streams at the foot of declivities, where the down thrust of the glaciers was heaviest, do we find lakes of considerable size and depth. How grateful a task it would be to trace them all and study them! How pure their waters are, clear as crystal in polished stone basins! None of them, so far as I have seen, have fishes, I suppose on account of falls making them inaccessible. Yet one would think their eggs might get into these lakes by some chance or other; on ducks' feet, for example, or in their mouths, or in their crops, as some plant seeds are distributed. Nature has so many ways of doing such things. How did the frogs, found in all the bogs and pools and lakes, however high, manage to get up these mountains? Surely not by jumping. Such excursions through miles of dry brush and boulders would be very hard on frogs. Perhaps their stringy gelatinous spawn is occasionally entangled or glued on the feet of water birds. Anyhow, they are here and in hearty health and voice. I like their cheery tronk and crink. They take the place of songbirds at a pinch.

August 11

Fine shining weather, with a ten minutes' noon thunderstorm and rain. Rambling all day getting acquainted with the region north of the river. Found a small lake and many charming glacier meadows embosomed in an extensive forest of the two-leaved pine. The forest is growing on broad, almost continuous deposits of moraine material, is remarkably even in its growth, and the trees are much closer together than in any of the fir or pine woods farther down the range. The evenness of the growth would seem to indicate that the trees are all of the same age or nearly so. This regularity has probably been in

great part the result of fire. I saw several large patches and strips of dead bleached spars, the ground beneath them covered with a young even growth. Fire can run in these woods, not only because the thin bark of the trees is dripping with resin, but because the growth is close, and the comparatively rich soil produces good crops of tall broad-leaved grasses on which fire can travel, even when the weather is calm. Besides these fire-killed patches there are a good many fallen uprooted trees here and there, some with the bark and needles still on, as if they had lately been blown down in some thunderstorm blast. Saw a large black-tailed deer, a buck with antlers like the upturned roots of a fallen pine.

After a long ramble through the dense encumbered woods I emerged upon a smooth meadow full of sunshine like a lake of light, about a mile and a half long, a quarter to half a mile wide, and bounded by tall arrowy pines. The sod, like that of all the glacier meadows hereabouts, is made of silky agrostis and calamagrostis chiefly; their panicles of purple flowers and purple stems, exceedingly light and airy, seem to float above the green plush of leaves like a thin misty cloud, while the sod is brightened by several species of gentian, potentilla, ivesia, orthocarpus, and their corresponding bees and butterflies. All the glacier meadows are beautiful, but few are so perfect as this one. Compared with it the most carefully leveled, licked, snipped artificial lawns of pleasure-grounds are coarse things. . . .

From meadow to meadow, every one beautiful beyond telling, and from lake to lake through groves and belts of arrowy trees, I held my way northward. . . .

August 12

. . . Moved camp to the side of the glacier meadow mentioned above. To let sheep trample so divinely fine a place seems barbarous. Fortunately they prefer the succulent broadleaved triticum and other woodland grasses to the silky species of the meadows, and therefore seldom bite them or set foot on them.

The shepherd and the Don cannot agree about methods of herding. Billy sets his dog Jack on the sheep far too often, so the Don thinks; and after some dispute to-day, in which the shepherd loudly claimed the right to dog the sheep as often as he pleased, he started for the plains. Now I suppose the care of the sheep will fall on me, though Mr. Delaney promises to do the herding himself for a while, then return to the lowlands and bring another shepherd, so as to leave me free to rove as I like. . . .

. . . Pushed northward beyond the forests to the head of the general basin, where traces of glacial action are strikingly clear and interesting. The recesses among the peaks look like quarries, so raw and fresh are the moraine chips and boulders that strew the ground in Nature's glacial workshops.

Soon after my return to camp we received a visit from an Indian, probably one of the hunters whose camp I had discovered. He came from Mono, he said, with others of his tribe, to hunt deer. One that he had killed a short distance from here he was carrying on his back, its legs tied together in an ornamental bunch on his forehead. Throwing down his burden, he gazed stolidly for a few minutes in silent Indian fashion, then cut off eight or ten pounds of venison for us, and begged a ''lill'' (little) of everything he saw or could think of—flour, bread, sugar, tobacco, whiskey, needles, etc. We gave a fair price for the meat in flour and sugar and added a few needles. A strange dirty and irregular life these dark-eyed, dark-haired, half-happy savages lead in this clean wilderness, —starvation and abundance, deathlike calm, indolence, and admirable, indefatigable action succeeding each other in stormy rhythm like winter and summer. Two things they have that civilized toilers might well envy them— pure air and pure water. . . .

August 13

Day all sunshine, dawn and evening purple, noon gold, no clouds, air motionless. Mr. Delaney arrived with two shepherds, one of them an Indian. On his way up from the plains he left some provisions at the Portuguese camp on Porcupine Creek near our old Yosemite camp, and I set out this morning with one of the pack animals to fetch them. Arrived at the Porcupine camp at noon, and might

have returned to the Tuolumne late in the evening, but concluded to stay over night with the Portuguese shepherds at their pressing invitation. They had sad stories to tell of losses from the Yosemite bears, and were so discouraged they seemed on the point of leaving the mountains; for the bears came every night and helped themselves to one or several of the flock in spite of all their efforts to keep them off.

I spent the afternoon in a grand ramble along the Yosemite walls. From the highest of the rocks called the Three Brothers, I enjoyed a magnificent view comprehending all the upper half of the floor of the valley and nearly all the rocks of the walls on both sides and at the head, with snowy peaks in the background. Saw also the Vernal and Nevada Falls, a truly glorious picture,—rocky strength and permanence combined with beauty of plants frail and fine and evanescent; water descending in thunder, and the same water gliding through meadows and groves in gentlest beauty. This standpoint is about eight thousand feet above the sea, or four thousand feet above the floor of the valley, and every tree, though looking small and feathery, stands in admirable clearness, and the shadows they cast are as distinct in outline as if seen at a distance of a few yards. They appeared even more so. No words will ever describe the exquisite beauty and charm of this mountain park—Nature's landscape garden at once tenderly beautiful and sublime. No wonder it draws nature-lovers from all over the world.

Glacial action even on this lofty summit is plainly displayed. Not only has all the lovely valley now smiling in sunshine been filled to the brim with ice, but it has been deeply overflowed.

"... The Vernal, four hundred feet high and about seventy-five or eighty feet wide, drops smoothly over a round-lipped precipice and forms a superb apron of embroidery, green and white, slightly folded and fluted, maintaining this form nearly to the bottom, where it is suddenly veiled in quick-flying billows of spray and mist, in which the afternoon sunbeams play with ravishing beauty of rainbow colors."

I visited our old Yosemite camp-ground on the head of Indian Creek, and found it fairly patted and smoothed down with bear-tracks. The bears had eaten all the sheep that were smothered in the corral, and some of the grand animals must have died, for Mr. Delaney, before leaving camp, put a large quantity of poison in the carcasses. All sheep-men carry strychnine to kill coyotes, bears, and panthers, though neither coyotes nor panthers are at all numerous in the upper mountains. The little dog-like wolves are far more numerous in the foothill region and on the plains, where they find a better supply of food,— saw only one panther-track above eight thousand feet.

On my return after sunset to the Portuguese camp I found the shepherds greatly excited over the behavior of the bears that have learned to like mutton. "They are getting worse and worse," they lamented. Not willing to wait decently until after dark for their suppers, they come and kill and eat their fill in broad daylight. The evening before my arrival, when the two shepherds were leisurely driving the flock toward camp half an hour before sunset, a hungry bear came out of the chaparral within a few yards of them and shuffled deliberately toward the flock. "Portuguese Joe," who always carried a gun loaded with buckshot, fired excitedly, threw down his gun, fled to the nearest suitable tree, and climbed to a safe height without waiting to see the effect of his shot. His companion also ran, but said that he saw the bear rise on its hind legs and throw out its arms as if feeling for somebody, and then go into the brush as if wounded.

At another of their camps in this neighborhood, a bear with two cubs attacked the flock before sunset, just as they were approaching the corral. Joe promptly climbed a tree out of danger, while Antone, rebuking his companion for cowardice in abandoning his charge, said that he was not going to let bears "eat up his sheeps" in daylight, and rushed towards the bears, shouting and setting his dog on them. The frightened cubs climbed a tree, but the mother ran to meet the shepherd and seemed anxious to fight. Antone stood astonished for a moment, eyeing the oncoming bear, then turned and fled, closely pursued. Unable to reach a suitable tree for climbing, he ran to the camp and scrambled up to the roof of the little cabin; the bear followed, but did not climb to the roof,—only stood glaring up at him for a few minutes, threatening him and holding him in mortal terror, then went to her cubs, called them down, went to the flock, caught a sheep for supper, and vanished in the brush. As soon as the bear left the cabin, the trembling Antone begged Joe to show him a good safe tree, up which he climbed like a sailor climb-ing a mast, and remained as long as he could hold on, the tree being almost branchless. After these disastrous experiences the two shepherds chopped and gathered large piles of dry wood and made a ring of fire around the corral every night, while one with a gun kept watch from a comfortable stage built on a neighboring pine that commanded a view of the corral. This evening the show made by the circle of fire was very fine, bringing out the surrounding trees in most impressive relief, and making the thousands of sheep eyes glow like a glorious bed of diamonds.

August 14

Up to the time I went to bed last night all was quiet, though we expected the shaggy freebooters every minute. They did not come till near midnight, when a pair walked boldly to the corral between two of the great fires, climbed in, killed two sheep and smothered ten, while the frightened watcher in the tree did not fire a single shot, saying that he was afraid he might kill some of the sheep, for the bears got into the corral before he got a good clear view of them. I told the shepherds they should at once move the flock to another camp. "Oh, no use, no use," they lamented; "where we go, the bears go too. See my poor dead sheeps—soon all dead. No use try another camp. We go down to the plains." And as I afterwards learned, they were driven out of the mountains a month before the usual time. Were bears much more numerous and destructive, the sheep would be kept away altogether. . . .

On the way back to our Tuolumne camp, I enjoyed the scenery if possible more than when it first came to view. Every feature already seems familiar as if I had lived here always. I never weary gazing at the wonderful Cathedral. It has more individual character than any other rock or mountain I ever saw, excepting perhaps the Yosemite South Dome. The forests, too, seem kindly familiar, and the lakes and meadows and glad singing streams. I should like to dwell with them forever. Here with bread and water I should be content. Even if not allowed to roam and climb, tethered to a stake or tree in some meadow or grove, even then I should be content forever. Bathed in such beauty, watching the expressions ever varying on the faces of the mountains, watching the stars, which here have a glory that the lowlander never dreams of, watching the circling seasons, listening to the songs of the waters and winds and birds, would be endless pleasure. And what glorious cloudlands I should see, storms and calms,—a new heaven and a new earth every day.

Up to the Highest Sierra

". . . Through a meadow opening in the pine woods I
see snowy peaks about the headwaters . . . How near they
seem and how clear their outlines on the blue air, or
rather *in* the blue air; for they seem to be saturated
with it. . . ."

" From garden to garden, ridge to ridge, I drifted enchanted, . . . gazing afar over domes and peaks, lakes and woods, and the billowy glaciated fields . . . In the midst of such beauty, pierced with its rays, one's body is all one tingling palate. Who wouldn't be a mountaineer!"

"... Small lakes abound in all sorts of situations,—on ridges, along mountain sides, and in piles of moraine boulders, most of them mere pools. . . . How pure their waters are, clear as crystal in polished stone basins!"

". . . These meadows are now in their prime. How wonderful must be the temper of the elastic leaves of grasses and sedges to make curves so perfect and fine. . . . All the glacier meadows are beautiful, but few are so perfect as this one. Compared with it the most carefully leveled, licked, snipped artificial lawns of pleasure-grounds are coarse things."

"Glacial lakes . . . strung together like beads on the bright ribbons of their feeding-streams, . . . pour, white and gray with foam and spray, from one to the other, their perfect mirror stillness making impressive contrasts with the grand blare and glare of the connecting cataracts."

"... The trees ... seem unable to go a step farther; but
up and up, far above the tree-line, these tender plants
climb, cheerily spreading their gray and pink carpets right
up to the very edges of the snowbanks in deep hollows
and shadows."

". . . How deeply with beauty is beauty overlaid! the
ground covered with crystals, the crystals with mosses and
lichens and low-spreading grasses and flowers, these with
large plants leaf over leaf with ever-changing color and
form, the broad palms of the firs outspread over these, the
azure dome over all like a bell-flower, and star above star."

". . . And our first pure mountain day, warm, calm, cloudless,—how immeasurable it seems, how serenely wild! I can scarcely remember its beginning. Along the river, over the hills, in the ground, in the sky, spring work is going on . . . new life, new beauty, unfolding, unrolling in glorious exuberant extravagance."

"When a mountain lake is born,—when, like a young eye, it first opens to the light,—it is an irregular, expressionless crescent, inclosed in banks of rock and ice . . ."

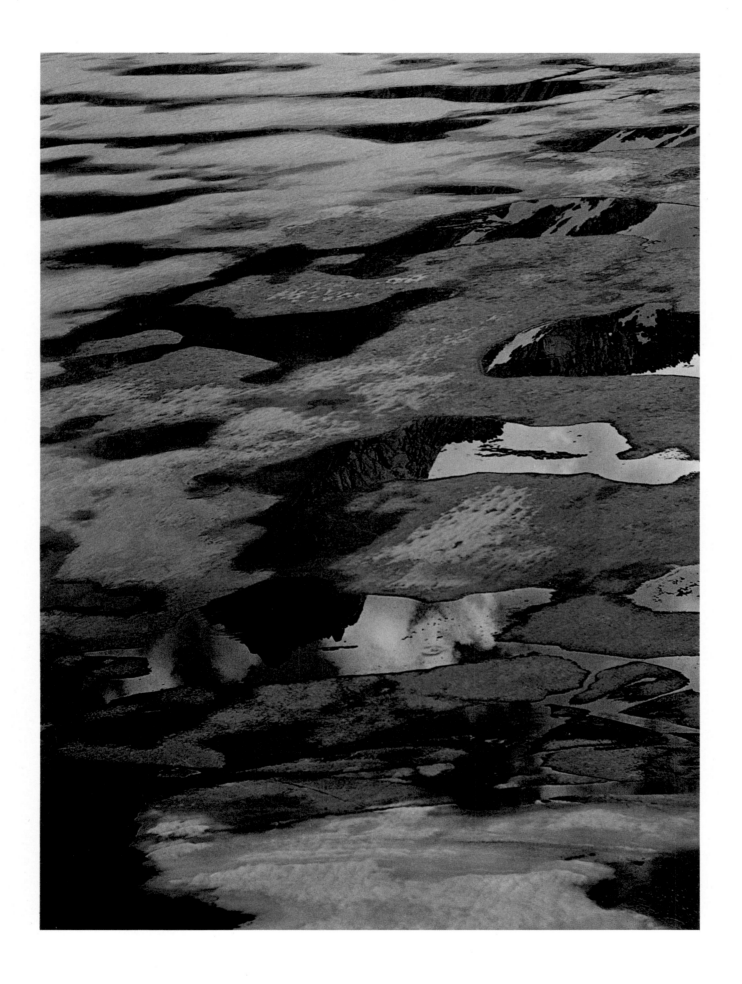

". . . Great banks of snow and ice are piled in hollows
on the cool precipitous north side . . ."

" . . . How boundless the
day seems as we revel in these storm-beaten sky gardens
amid so vast a congregation of onlooking mountains!"

". . . The grass of the meadows is mostly fine and silky,
with exceedingly slender leaves, making a close sod, above
which the panicles of minute purple flowers seem to float
in airy, misty lightness . . ."

Bloody Canyon and Mono Lake

August 21

Have just returned from a fine wild excursion across the range to Mono Lake, by way of the Mono or Bloody Canyon Pass. Mr. Delaney has been good to me all summer, lending a helping, sympathizing hand at every opportunity, as if my wild notions and rambles and studies were his own. He is one of those remarkable California men who have been overflowed and denuded and remodeled by the excitements of the gold fields, like the Sierra landscapes by grinding ice, bringing the harder bosses and ridges of character into relief,—a tall, lean, big-boned, big-hearted Irishman, educated for a priest in Maynooth College,—lots of good in him, shining out now and then in this mountain light. Recognizing my love of wild places, he told me one evening that I ought to go through Bloody Canyon, for he was sure I should find it wild enough. He had not been there himself, he said, but had heard many of his mining friends speak of it as the wildest of all the Sierra passes. Of course I was glad to go. It lies just to the east of our camp and swoops down from the summit of the range to the edge of the Mono Desert, making a descent of about four thousand feet in a distance of about four miles. It was known and traveled as a pass by wild animals and the Indians long before its discovery by white men in the gold year of 1858, as is shown by old trails which come together at the head of it. The name may have been suggested by the red color of the metamorphic slates in which the canyon abounds, or by the blood stains on the rocks from the unfortunate animals that were compelled to slide and shuffle over the sharp-angled boulders.

Early in the morning I tied my notebook and some bread to my belt, and strode away full of eager hope, feeling that I was going to have a glorious revel. The glacier meadows that lay along my way served to soothe my morning speed, for the sod was full of blue gentians and daisies, kalmia and dwarf vaccinium, calling for recognition as old friends, and I had to stop many times to examine the shining rocks over which the ancient glacier had passed with tremendous pressure, polishing them so well that they reflected the sunlight like glass in some places, while fine striæ, seen clearly through a lens, indicated the direction in which the ice had flowed. On some of the sloping polished pavements abrupt steps occur, showing that occasionally large masses of the rock had given way before the glacial pressure, as well as small particles; moraines, too, some scattered, others regular like long curving embankments and dams, occur here and there, giving the general surface of the region a young, new-made appearance. I watched the gradual dwarfing of the pines as I ascended, and the corresponding dwarfing of nearly all the rest of the vegetation. On the slopes of Mammoth Mountain, to the south of the pass, I saw many gaps in the woods reaching from the upper edge of the timberline down to the level meadows, where avalanches of snow had descended, sweeping away every tree in their paths as well as the soil they were growing in, leaving the bedrock bare. The trees are nearly all uprooted, but a few that had been extremely well anchored in clefts of the rock were broken off near the ground. It seems strange at first sight that trees that had been allowed to grow for a century or more undisturbed should in their old age be thus swished away at a stroke. Such avalanches can only occur under rare conditions of weather and snowfall. No doubt on some positions of the mountain slopes the inclination and smoothness of the surface is such that avalanches must occur every winter, or even after every heavy snowstorm, and of course no trees or even bushes can grow in their channels. I noticed a few clean-swept slopes of this kind. The uprooted trees that had grown in the pathway of what might be called "century avalanches" were piled in windrows, and tucked snugly against the wall-trees of the gaps, heads downward, excepting a few that were carried out into the open ground of the meadows, where the heads of the avalanches had stopped. Young pines, mostly the two-leaved and the white-barked, are already springing up in these cleared gaps. It would be interesting to ascertain the age of these saplings, for thus we should gain a fair approximation to the year that the great avalanches occurred. Perhaps most or all of them occurred the same winter. . . .

Near the summit at the head of the pass I found a species of dwarf willow lying perfectly flat on the ground, making a nice, soft, silky gray carpet, not a single stem or branch more than three inches high; but the catkins, which are now nearly ripe, stand erect and make a close, nearly regular gray growth, being larger than all the rest of the plants. Some of these interesting dwarfs have only one catkin — willow bushes reduced to their lowest terms. . . . The trees, tough and resiny, seem unable to go a step farther; but up and up, far above the tree-line, these tender plants climb, cheerily spreading their gray and pink carpets right up to the very edges of the snow-banks in deep hollows and shadows. . . . I at length entered the gate of the pass, and the huge rocks began to close around me in all their mysterious impressiveness. . . .

At sundown the somber crags and peaks were inspired with the ineffable beauty of the alpenglow, and a solemn, awful stillness hushed everything in the landscape. Then I crept into a hollow by the side of a small lake near the head of the canyon, smoothed a sheltered spot, and gathered a few pine tassels for a bed. After the short twilight began to fade I kindled a sunny fire, made a tin cupful of tea, and lay down to watch the stars. Soon the night-wind began to flow from the snowy peaks overhead, at first only a gentle breathing, then gaining strength, in less than an hour rumbled in massive volume something like a boisterous stream in a boulder-choked channel, roaring and moaning down the canyon as if the work it had to do was tremendously important and fateful; and mingled with these storm tones were those of the water-falls on the north side of the canyon, now sounding dis-tinctly, now smothered by the heavier cataracts of air, making a glorious psalm of savage wildness. My fire squirmed and struggled as if ill at ease, for though in a sheltered nook, detached masses of icy wind often fell like icebergs on top of it, scattering sparks and coals, so that I had to keep well back to avoid being burned. But the big resiny roots and knots of the dwarf pine could neither be beaten out nor blown away, and the flames, now rush-ing up in long lances, now flattened and twisted on the rocky ground, roared as if trying to tell the storm stories of the trees they belonged to, as the light given out was telling the story of the sunshine they had gathered in centuries of summers.

The stars shone clear in the strip of sky between the huge dark cliffs; and as I lay recalling the lessons of the day, suddenly the full moon looked down over the canyon wall, her face apparently filled with eager concern, which had a startling effect, as if she had left her place in the sky and had come down to gaze on me alone, like a person entering one's bedroom. It was hard to realize that she was in her place in the sky, and was looking abroad on half the globe, land and sea, mountains, plains, lakes, rivers, oceans, ships, cities with their myriads of inhabi-tants sleeping and waking, sick and well. No, she seemed to be just on the rim of Bloody Canyon and looking only at me. This was indeed getting near to Nature. I remember watching the harvest moon rising above the oak trees in Wisconsin apparently as big as a cart-wheel and not farther than half a mile distant. With these exceptions I might say I never before had seen the moon, and this night she seemed so full of life and so near, the effect was marvel-ously impressive and made me forget the Indians, the great black rocks above me, and the wild uproar of the winds and waters making their way down the huge jagged gorge. . . . I slept but little and gladly welcomed the dawn over the Mono Desert. . . . I set forth, gazing eagerly at the tremendous walls of red slates savagely hacked and scarred and apparently ready to fall in avalanches great enough to choke the pass and fill up the chain of lakelets. But soon its beauties came to view, and I bounded lightly from rock to rock, admiring the polished bosses shining in the slant sunshine with glorious effect in the general roughness of moraines and avalanche taluses, even toward the head of the canyon near the highest fountains of the ice. Here, too, are most of the lowly plant people seen yesterday on the other side of the divide now opening their beautiful eyes. None could fail to glory in Nature's tender care for them in so wild a place. The little ouzel is flitting from rock to rock along the rapid swirling Canyon Creek, diving for breakfast in icy pools, and merrily singing as if the huge rugged avalanche-swept gorge was the most delightful of all its mountain homes. Besides a high fall on the north wall of the canyon, apparently coming direct from the sky, there are many narrow cascades, bright silvery rib-bons zigzagging down the red cliffs, tracing the diagonal cleavage joints of the metamorphic slates, now contracted and out of sight, now leaping from ledge to ledge in filmy sheets. . . . And on the main Canyon Creek, to which all these are tributary, is a series of small falls, cascades, and rapids extending all the way down to the foot of the canyon, interrupted only by the lakes in which the tossed and beaten waters rest. One of the finest of the cascades is outspread on the face of a precipice, its waters separated into ribbon-like strips, and woven into a dia-mond-like pattern by tracing the cleavage joints of the rock, while tufts of bryanthus, grass, sedge, saxifrage form beautiful fringes. Who could imagine beauty so fine in so savage a place?

One of the smallest of the cascades, which I name the

Bower Cascade, is in the lower region of the pass, where the vegetation is snowy and luxuriant. Wild rose and dogwood form dense masses overarching the stream, and out of this bower the creek, grown strong with many indashing tributaries, leaps forth into the light, and descends in a fluted curve thick-sown with crisp flashing spray. At the foot of the canyon there is a lake formed in part at least by the damming of the stream by a terminal moraine. The three other lakes in the canyon are in basins eroded from the solid rock, where the pressure of the glacier was greatest, and the most resisting portions of the basin rims are beautifully, tellingly polished. Below Moraine Lake at the foot of the canyon there are several old lake-basins lying between the large lateral moraines which extend out into the desert. These basins are now completely filled up by the material carried in by the streams, and changed to dry sandy flats covered mostly by grass and artemisia and sun-loving flowers. All these lower lake-basins were evidently formed by terminal moraine dams deposited where the receding glacier had lingered during short periods of less waste, or greater snowfall, or both.

Looking up the canyon from the warm sunny edge of the Mono plain my morning ramble seems a dream, so great is the change in the vegetation and climate. The lilies on the bank of Moraine Lake are higher than my head, and the sunshine is hot enough for palms. Yet the snow round the arctic gardens at the summit of the pass is plainly visible, only about four miles away, and between lie specimen zones of all the principal climates of the globe. In little more than an hour one many swoop down from winter to summer, from an Arctic to a torrid region, through as great changes of climate as one would encounter in traveling from Labrador to Florida.

The Indians I had met near the head of the canyon had camped at the foot of it the night before they made the ascent, and I found their fire still smoking on the side of a small tributary stream near Moraine Lake; and on the edge of what is called the Mono Desert, four or five miles from the lake, I came to a patch of elymus, or wild rye, growing in magnificent waving clumps six or eight feet high, bearing heads six to eight inches long. The crop was ripe, and Indian women were gathering the grain in baskets by bending down large handfuls, beating out the seed, and fanning it in the wind. The grains are about five eighths of an inch long, dark-colored and sweet. I fancy the bread made from it must be as good as wheat bread. . . . Down on the shore of Mono Lake I saw a number of their flimsy huts on the banks of streams that dash swiftly into that dead sea,—mere brush tents where they lie and eat at their ease. Some of the men were feasting on buffalo berries,

lying beneath the tall bushes now red with fruit. The berries are rather insipid, but they must needs be wholesome, since for days and weeks the Indians, it is said, eat nothing else. In the season they in like manner depend chiefly on the fat larvæ of a fly that breeds in the salt water of the lake, or on the big fat corrugated caterpillars of a species of silkworm that feeds on the leaves of the yellow pine. Occasionally a grand rabbit-drive is organized and hundreds are slain with clubs on the lake shore, chased and frightened into a dense crowd by dogs, boys, girls, men and women, and rings of sage brush fire, when of course they are quickly killed. The skins are made into blankets. In the autumn the more enterprising of the hunters bring in a good many deer, and rarely a wild sheep from the high peaks. Antelopes used to be abundant on the desert at the base of the interior mountain-ranges. Sage hens, grouse, and squirrels help to vary their wild diet of worms; pine nuts also from the small interesting *Pinus monophylla,* and good bread and good mush are made from acorns and wild rye. Strange to say, they seem to like the lake larvæ best of all. Long windrows are washed up on the shore, which they gather and dry like grain for winter use. It is said that wars, on account of encroachments on each other's worm-grounds, are of common occurrence among the various tribes and families. Each claims a certain marked portion of the shore. The pine nuts are delicious—large quantities are gathered every autumn. The tribes of the west flank of the range trade acorns for worms and pine nuts. The squaws carry immense loads on their backs across the rough passes and down the range, making journeys of about forty or fifty miles each way.

The desert around the lake is surprisingly flowery. In many places among the sage bushes I saw mentzelia, abronia, aster, bigelovia, and gilia, all of which seemed to enjoy the hot sunshine. . . .

Opposite the mouth of the canyon a range of volcanic cones extends southward from the lake, rising abruptly out of the desert like a chain of mountains. The largest of the cones are about twenty-five hundred feet high above the lake level, have well-formed craters, and all of them are evidently comparatively recent additions to the landscape. At a distance of a few miles they look like heaps of loose ashes that have never been blest by either rain or snow. . . . A country of wonderful contrasts. Hot deserts bounded by snow-laden mountains,—cinders and ashes scattered on glacier-polished pavements,—frost and fire working together in the making of beauty. In the lake are several volcanic islands, which show that the waters were once mingled with fire.

Along the East Side of the Crest

"... the sunshine is hot enough for palms. Yet the snow round the arctic gardens at the summit of the pass is plainly visible, only about four miles away, and between lie specimen zones of all the principal climates of the globe."

"...Down on the shore of Mono Lake I saw a number of streams that dash swiftly into the dead sea... The lake, eight or ten miles in diameter, shines like a burnished disk of silver, no trees about its gray, ashy, cindery shores.... Opposite the mouth of the canyon a range of volcanic cones extends southward from the lake, rising abruptly out of the desert like a chain of mountains . . . well-formed craters, and all of them are evidently comparatively recent additions to the landscape.

"... Who could imagine beauty so fine in so savage a place? Gardens are blooming in all sorts of nooks and hollows ..."

"The highest and youngest of all the lakes lie nestled in glacier wombs. At first sight, they seem pictures of pure bloodless desolation, miniature arctic seas, bound in perpetual ice and snow, and overshadowed by harsh, gloomy, crumbling precipices. Their waters are keen ultramarine blue in the deepest parts, lively grass-green toward the shore shallows and around the edges of the small bergs usually floating about in them."

"... the radiant host of trees stand hushed and thoughtful, receiving the Sun's good-night, as solemn and impressive a leave-taking as if sun and trees were to meet no more. The daylight fades, the color spell is broken, and the forest breathes free in the night breeze beneath the stars."

"... Looking northward and southward along the axis of the range, you see the glorious array of high mountains, crags and peaks and snow, the fountain-heads of rivers that are flowing west to the sea . . . and east to hot salt lakes and deserts to evaporate and hurry back into the sky."

"This grand show is eternal.
It is always sunrise somewhere;
the dew is never all dried at once;
a shower is forever falling; vapor is ever rising.
Eternal sunrise, eternal sunset, eternal dawn and gloaming,
on sea and continents and islands, each in its turn,
as the round earth rolls."

Glad to get back to the green side of the mountains, though I have greatly enjoyed the gray east side and hope to see more of it. Reading these grand mountain manuscripts displayed through every vicissitude of heat and cold, calm and storm, upheaving volcanoes and down-grinding glaciers, we see that everything in Nature called destruction must be creation—a change from beauty to beauty.

Our glacier meadow camp north of the Soda Springs seems more beautiful every day. The grass covers all the ground though the leaves are thread-like in fineness, and in walking on the sod it seems like a plush carpet of marvelous richness and softness, and the purple panicles brushing against one's feet are not felt. This is a typical glacier meadow, occupying the basin of a vanished lake, very definitely bounded by walls of the arrowy two-leaved pines drawn up in a handsome orderly array like soldiers on parade. There are many other meadows of the same kind hereabouts imbedded in the woods. The main big meadows along the river are the same in general and extend with but little interruption for ten or twelve miles, but none I have seen are so finely finished and perfect as this one. It is richer in flowering plants than the prairies of Wisconsin and Illinois were when in all their wild glory. The showy flowers are mostly three species of gentian, a purple and yellow orthocarpus, a golden-rod or two, a small blue pentstemon almost like a gentian, potentilla, ivesia, pedicularis, white violet, kalmia, and bryanthus. There are no coarse weedy plants. Through this flowery lawn flows a stream silently gliding, swirling, slipping as if careful not to make the slightest noise. It is only about three feet wide in most places, widening here and there into pools six or eight feet in diameter with no apparent current, the banks bossily rounded by the down-curving mossy sod, grass panicles over-leaning like miniature pine trees, and rugs of bryanthus spreading here and there over sunken boulders. At the foot of the meadow the stream, rich with the juices of the plants it has refreshed, sings merrily down over shelving rock ledges on its way to the Tuolumne River. The sublime, massive Mount Dana and its companions, green, red, and white, loom impressively above the pines along the eastern horizon; a range or spur of gray rugged granite crags and mountains on the north; the curiously crested and battlemented Mount Hoffmann on the west; and the Cathedral Range on the south with its grand Cathedral Peak, Cathedral Spires, Unicorn Peak, and several others, gray and pointed or massively rounded.

". . . Bathed in such beauty, watching the expressions ever varying on the faces of the mountains, watching the stars, which here have a glory that the lowlander never dreams of, watching the circling seasons, listening to the songs of the waters and winds and birds, would be endless pleasure. And what glorious cloudlands I should see, storms and calms,—a new heaven and a new earth every day."

The Tuolumne Camp

August 23

Cool, bright day, hinting Indian summer. . . .

Rose and crimson sunset, and soon after the stars appeared the moon rose in most impressive majesty over the top of Mount Dana. I sauntered up the meadow in the white light. The jet-black tree-shadows were so wonderfully distinct and substantial looking, I often stepped high in crossing them, taking them for black charred logs.

August 24

. . . Slight frost, Indian summerish, the mountains growing softer in outline and dreamy looking, their rough angles melted off, apparently. Sky at evening with fine, dark, subdued purple, almost like the evening purple of the San Joaquin plains in settled weather. The moon is now gazing over the summit of Dana. Glorious exhilarating air. I wonder if in all the world there is another mountain range of equal height blessed with weather so fine, and so openly kind and hospitable and approachable.

August 25

Cool as usual in the morning, quickly changing to the ordinary serene generous warmth and brightness. Toward evening the west wind was cool and sent us to the campfire. Of all Nature's flowery carpeted mountain halls none can be finer than this glacier meadow. Bees and butterflies seem as abundant as ever. The birds are still here, showing no sign of leaving for winter quarters though the frost must bring them to mind. For my part I should like to stay here all winter or all my life or even all eternity.

August 26

Frost this morning; all the meadow grass and some of the pine needles sparkling with irised crystals,—flowers of light. Large picturesque clouds, craggy like rocks, are piled on Mount Dana, reddish in color like the mountain itself; the sky for a few degrees around the horizon is pale purple, into which the pines dip their spires with fine effect. Spent the day as usual looking about me, watching the changing lights, the ripening autumn colors of the grass, seeds, late-blooming gentians, asters, goldenrods; parting the meadow grass here and there and looking down into the underworld of mosses and liverworts; . . . studying the formation of lakes and meadows, moraines, mountain sculpture; making small beginnings in these directions, charmed by the serene beauty of everything.

The day has been extra cloudy, though bright on the whole, for the clouds were brighter than common. Clouds about .15, which in Switzerland would be considered extra clear. Probably more free sunshine falls on this majestic range than on any other in the world I've ever seen or heard of. It has the brightest weather, brightest glacier-polished rocks, the greatest abundance of irised spray from its glorious waterfalls, the brightest forests of silver firs and silver pines, more starshine, moonshine, and perhaps more crystalshine than any other mountain chain, and its countless mirror lakes, having more light poured into them, glow and spangle most. And how glorious the shining after the short summer showers and after frosty nights when the morning sunbeams are pouring through the crystals on the grass and pine needles, and how ineffably spiritually fine is the morning-glow on the mountain-tops and the alpenglow of evening. Well may the Sierra be named, not the Snowy Range, but the Range of Light.

August 27

. . . Contemplating the lace-like fabric of streams outspread over the mountains, we are reminded that everything is flowing—going somewhere, animals and so-called lifeless rocks as well as water. Thus the snow flows fast or slow in grand beauty-making glaciers and avalanches; the air in majestic floods carrying minerals, plant leaves, seeds, spores, with streams of music and fragrance; water streams carrying rocks both in solution and in the form of mud particles, sand, pebbles, and boulders. Rocks flow from volcanoes like water from springs, and animals flock together and flow in currents modified by stepping, leaping, gliding, flying, swimming, etc. While the stars go streaming through space pulsed on and on forever. . . .

August 28

. . . A fine crop of hoarfrost. Warm after ten o'clock. The gentians don't mind the first frost though their petals seem so delicate; they close every night as if going to sleep, and awake fresh as ever in the morning sun-glory. The grass is a shade browner since last week, but there are no nipped wilted plants of any sort as far as I have seen. Butterflies and the grand host of smaller flies are benumbed every night, but they hover and dance in the sunbeams over the meadows before noon with no apparent lack of playful, joyful life. Soon they must all fall like petals in an orchard, dry and wrinkled, not a wing of all the mighty host left to tingle the air. Nevertheless new myriads will arise in the spring. . . .

August 29

. . . Have been gazing all day at the mountains, watching the changing lights. More and more plainly are they clothed with light as a garment, white tinged with pale purple, palest during the midday hours, richest in the morning and evening. . . .

August 30

. . . Frost enough for crystal building,—glorious fields of ice-diamonds destined to last but a night. How lavish is Nature building, pulling down, creating, destroying, chasing every material particle from form to form, ever changing, ever beautiful. . . .

August 31

. . . Frost enough for another crop of crystals on the meadows but none on the forests. The gentians, golden-rods, asters, etc., don't seem to feel it; neither petals nor leaves are touched though they seem so tender. Every day opens and closes like a flower, noiseless, effortless. . . .

September 1

. . . Have been up Mount Dana, making haste to see as much as I can now that the time of departure is drawing nigh. The views from the summit reach far and wide, eastward over the Mono Lake and Desert; mountains beyond mountains looking strangely barren and gray and bare like heaps of ashes dumped from the sky. The lake, eight or ten miles in diameter, shines like a burnished disk of silver, no trees about its gray, ashy, cindery shores. Looking westward, the glorious forests are seen sweeping over countless ridges and hills, girdling domes and subordinate mountains, fringing in long curving lines the dividing ridges, and filling every hollow where the glaciers have spread soil-beds however rocky or smooth. Looking northward and southward along the axis of the range, you see the glorious array of high mountains, crags and peaks and snow, the fountain-heads of rivers that are flowing

west to the sea through the famous Golden Gate, and east to hot salt lakes and deserts to evaporate and hurry back into the sky. Innumerable lakes are shining like eyes beneath heavy rock brows, bare or tree fringed, or imbedded in black forests. Meadow openings in the woods seem as numerous as the lakes or perhaps more so. Far up the moraine-covered slopes and among crumbling rocks I found many delicate hardy plants, some of them still in flower. The best gains of this trip were the lessons of unity and inter-relation of all the features of the landscape revealed in general views. The lakes and meadows are located

Glacier meadow strewn with moraine boulders
Elevation 10,000 feet near Mount Dana

just where the ancient glaciers bore heaviest at the foot of the steepest parts of their channels, and of course their longest diameters are approximately parallel with each other and with the belts of forests growing in long curving lines on the lateral and medial moraines, and in broad outspreading fields on the terminal beds deposited toward the end of the ice period when the glaciers were receding. . . . The bread camp must soon be removed. If I had a few sacks of flour, an axe, and some matches, I would build a cabin of pine logs, pile up plenty of firewood about it and stay all winter to see the grand fertile snow-storms, watch the birds and animals that winter thus high, how they live, how the forests look snow-laden or buried, and how the avalanches look and sound on their way down the mountains. But now I'll have to go, for there is nothing to spare in the way of provisions. I'll surely be back, however, surely I'll be back. No other place has ever so overwhelmingly attracted me. . . .

September 2

. . . the first marked change from tranquil sunshine with purple mornings and evenings and still, white noons. There is nothing like a storm, however. . . . no sighing in the woods to betoken a big weather change. The sky was red in the morning and evening, the color not diffused like the ordinary purple glow, but loaded upon separate well-defined clouds that remained motionless, as if anchored around the jagged mountain-fenced horizon. A deep-red cap, bluffy around its sides, lingered a long time on Mount Dana and Mount Gibbs, drooping so low as to hide most of their bases, but leaving Dana's round summit free, which seemed to float separate and alone over the big crimson cloud. . . . One is constantly reminded of the infinite lavishness and fertility of Nature—inexhaustible abundance amid what seems enormous waste. And yet when we look into any of her operations that lie within reach of our minds, we learn that no particle of her material is wasted or worn out. It is eternally flowing from use to use, beauty to yet higher beauty. . . .

September 4

All the vast sky dome is clear, filled only with mellow Indian summer light. The pine and hemlock and fir cones are nearly ripe and are falling fast from morning to night, cut off and gathered by the busy squirrels. Almost all the plants have matured their seeds, their summer work done; and the summer crop of birds and deer will soon be able to follow their parents to the foothills and plains at the approach of winter, when the snow begins to fly.

September 6

. . . Mr. Delaney now keeps up a solemn talk about the need of getting away from these high mountains, telling sad stories of flocks that perished in storms that broke suddenly into the midst of fine innocent weather like this we are now enjoying. "In no case," said he, "will I venture to stay so high and far back in the mountains as we now are later than the middle of this month, no matter how warm and sunny it may be." He would move the flock slowly at first, a few miles a day until the Yosemite Creek basin was reached and crossed, then while lingering in the heavy pine woods should the weather threaten he could hurry down to the foothills, where the snow never falls deep enough to smother a sheep. Of course I am anxious to see as much of the wilderness as possible in the few days left me, and I say again,—May the good time come when I can stay as long as I like with plenty of bread, far and free from trampling flocks. . . .

September 7

Left camp at daybreak and made direct for Cathedral Peak, intending to strike eastward and southward from that point among the peaks and ridges at the heads of the Tuolumne, Merced, and San Joaquin Rivers. Down through the pine woods I made my way, across the Tuol-

umne River and meadows, and up the heavily timbered slope forming the south boundary of the upper Tuolumne basin, along the east side of Cathedral Peak, and up to its topmost spire, which I reached at noon, having loitered by the way to study the fine trees—two-leaved pine, mountain pine, albicaulis pine, silver fir, and the most charming, most graceful of all the evergreens, the mountain hemlock. High, cool, late-flowering meadows also detained me, and lakelets and avalanche tracks and huge quarries of moraine rocks above the forests.

Front of Cathedral Peak

All the way up from the Big Meadows to the base of the Cathedral the ground is covered with moraine material, the left lateral moraine of the great glacier that must have completely filled this upper Tuolumne basin. Higher there are several small terminal moraines of residual glaciers shoved forward at right angles against the grand simple lateral of the main Tuolumne Glacier. A fine place to study mountain sculpture and soil making. The view from the Cathedral Spires is very fine and telling in every direction. Innumerable peaks, ridges, domes, meadows, lakes, and woods; the forests extending in long curving lines and broad fields wherever the glaciers have left soil for them to grow on, while the sides of the highest mountains show a straggling dwarf growth clinging to rifts in the rocks apparently independent of soil. The dark heath-like growth on the Cathedral roof I found to be dwarf snow-pressed albicaulis pine, about three or four feet high, but very old looking. Many of them are bearing cones, and the noisy Clarke crow is eating the seeds, using his long bill like a woodpecker in digging them out of the cones. A good many flowers are still in bloom about the base of the peak, and even on the roof among the little pines, especially a woody yellow-flowered eriogonum and a handsome aster. The body of the Cathedral is nearly square, and the roof slopes are wonderfully regular and symmetrical, the ridge trending northeast and southwest.

This direction has apparently been determined by structure joints in the granite. The gable on the northeast end is magnificent in size and simplicity, and at its base there is a big snow-bank protected by the shadow of the building. The front is adorned with many pinnacles and a tall spire of curious workmanship. Here too the joints in the

One of the highest Mount Ritter fountains

rock are seen to have played an important part in determining their forms and size and general arrangement. The Cathedral is said to be about eleven thousand feet above the sea, but the height of the building itself above the level of the ridge it stands on is about fifteen hundred feet. A mile or so to the westward there is a handsome lake, and the glacier-polished granite about it is shining so brightly it is not easy in some places to trace the line between the rock and water, both shining alike. Of this lake with its silvery basin and bits of meadow and groves I have a fine view from the spires; also of . . . the vast multitude of snowy fountain peaks extending far north and south along the axis of the range. No feature, however, of all the noble landscape as seen from here seems more wonderful than the Cathedral itself, a temple displaying Nature's best masonry and sermons in stones. . . . This I may say is the first time I have been at church in California, led here at last, every door graciously opened for the poor lonely worshiper. In our best times everything turns into religion, all the world seems a church and the mountains altars. . . . Camped beside a little pool and a group of crinkled dwarf pines; and as I sit by the fire trying to write notes the shallow pool seems fathomless with the infinite starry heavens in it. . . . And beyond the fire-beams out in the solemn darkness, how impressive is the music of a choir of rills singing their way down from the snow to the river! . . .

. . . Found a species of sedge in flower within eight or ten feet of a snow-bank. Judging by the looks of the ground, it can hardly have been out in the sunshine much longer than a week, and it is likely to be buried again in fresh snow in a month or so, thus making a winter about ten months long, while spring, summer, and autumn are crowded and hurried into two months. . . .

September 8

Day of climbing, scrambling, sliding on the peaks around the highest source of the Tuolumne and Merced. Climbed three of the most commanding of the mountains, whose names I don't know; crossed streams and huge beds of ice and snow more than I could keep count of. Neither could I keep count of the lakes scattered on table-lands and in the cirques of the peaks, and in chains in the canyons, linked together by the streams—a tremendously wild gray wilderness of hacked, shattered crags, ridges, and peaks, a few clouds drifting over and through the midst of them as if looking for work. . . . I must have done three or four days' climbing work in this one. Limbs

Upper Tuolumne Valley

perfectly tireless until near sundown, when I descended into the main upper Tuolumne valley at the foot of Mount Lyell, the camp still eight or ten miles distant. Going up through the pine woods past the Soda Springs Dome in the dark, where there is much fallen timber, and when all the excitement of seeing things was wanting, I was tired. Arrived at the main camp at nine o'clock, and soon was sleeping sound as death.

"When we try to pick out anything by itself, we find it hitched to everything else in the universe."

Back to the Lowlands

September 9

Weariness rested away and I feel eager and ready for another excursion a month or two long in the same wonderful wilderness. Now, however, I must turn toward the lowlands, praying and hoping Heaven will shove me back again.

The most telling thing learned in these mountain excursions is the influence of cleavage joints on the features sculptured from the general mass of the range. Evidently the denudation has been enormous, while the inevitable outcome is subtle balanced beauty. Comprehended in general views, the features of the wildest landscape seem to be as harmoniously related as the features of a human face. Indeed, they look human and radiate spiritual beauty, divine thought, however covered and concealed by rock and snow. . . .

. . . The camp stuff is now packed on the horses, and the flock is headed for the home ranch. Away we go, down through the pines, leaving the lovely lawn where we have camped so long. I wonder if I'll ever see it again. The sod is so tough and close it is scarcely at all injured by the sheep. Fortunately they are not fond of silky glacier meadow grass. The day is perfectly clear, not a cloud or the faintest hint of a cloud is visible, and there is no wind. I wonder if in all the world, at a height of nine thousand feet, weather so steadily, faithfully calm and bright and hospitable may anywhere else be found. We are going away fearing destructive storms, though it is difficult to conceive weather changes so great.

Though the water is now low in the river, the usual difficulty occurred in getting the flock across it. Every sheep seemed to be invincibly determined to die any sort of dry death rather than wet its feet. Carlo has learned the sheep business as perfectly as the best shepherd, and it is interesting to watch his intelligent efforts to push or frighten the silly creatures into the water. They had to be fairly crowded and shoved over the bank; and when at last one crossed because it could not push its way back, the whole flock suddenly plunged in headlong together, as if the river was the only desirable part of the world. Aside from mere money profit one would rather herd wolves than

sheep. As soon as they clambered up the opposite bank, they began baaing and feeding as if nothing unusual had happened. We crossed the meadows and drove slowly up the south rim of the valley through the same woods I had passed on my way to Cathedral Peak, and camped for the night by the side of a small pond on top of the big lateral moraine.

September 10-22

In the morning at daybreak not one of the two thousand sheep was in sight. Examining the tracks, we discovered that they had been scattered, perhaps by a bear. In a few hours all were found and gathered into one flock again. Had fine view of a deer. How graceful and perfect in every way it seemed as compared with the silly, dusty, tousled sheep! From the high ground hereabouts had another grand view to the northward—a heaving, swelling sea of domes and round-backed ridges fringed with pines, and bounded by innumerable sharp-pointed peaks, gray and barren-looking, though so full of beautiful life. Another day of the calm, cloudless kind, purple in the morning and evening. The evening glow has been very marked for the last two or three weeks. Perhaps the "zodiacal light."

Cloudless. Slight frost. Calm. Fairly started downhill, and now are camped at the west end meadows of Lake Tenaya. . . . Lake smooth as glass, mirroring its miles of glacier-polished pavements and bold mountain walls. Find aster still in flower. Here is about the upper limit of the dwarf form of the goldcup oak,—eight thousand feet above sea-level,—reaching about two thousand feet higher than the California black oak (*Quercus Californica*). Lovely evening, the lake reflections after dark marvelously impressive. . . .

Nearly all day in magnificent fir forest, the top branches laden with superb erect gray cones shining with beads of pure balsam. The squirrels are cutting them off at a great rate. Bump, bump, I hear them falling, soon to be gathered and stored for winter bread. . . . The sunset very rich, flaming purple and crimson showing gloriously through the aisles of the woods.

"The weather pure gold . . . white cirrus flects and pencilings around the horizon . . ."

". . . The forests we so admired in summer seem still more beautiful and sublime in this mellow autumn light. Lovely starry night, the tall, spiring tree-tops relieved in jet black against the sky. I linger by the fire, loath to go to bed."

"Climb the mountains and get their good tidings.
Nature's peace will flow into you
    as sunshine flows into trees.
The winds will blow their own freshness into you,
    and the storms their energy,
        while cares will drop off like autumn leaves."

"...Frost this morning; all the meadow grass and some of the pine needles sparkling with irised crystals,—flowers of light. . . . one of the cleanest landscapes in the world. How well it is washed! The sea is hardly less dusty than the ice-burnished pavements and ridges, domes and canyons. . . . No wonder the hills and groves were God's first temples . . .

"...For my part, I should like to stay here all winter or all my life or even all eternity."

"The last days of this glacial winter are not yet past, so young is our world. I used to envy the father of our race, dwelling as he did in contact with the new-made fields and plants of Eden; but I do so no more, because I have discovered that I also live in 'creation's dawn.' The morning stars still sing together, and the world, not yet half made, becomes more beautiful every day."

"These beautiful days must enrich all my life. They do not exist as mere pictures . . . but they saturate themselves into every part of the body and live always."

Here ends my forever memorable first High Sierra excursion. I have crossed the Range of Light, surely the brightest and best of all the Lord has built; and rejoicing in its glory, I gladly, gratefully, hopefully pray I may see it again.